The Warren Court

The Warren Court

CONSTITUTIONAL DECISION AS
AN INSTRUMENT OF REFORM

Archibald Cox

Harvard University Press
CAMBRIDGE, MASSACHUSETTS
LONDON, ENGLAND

Preface

THE APPOINTMENT OF Earl Warren as Chief Justice of the United States in 1953 marked the opening of a new period in our constitutional development. In the next fifteen years the Supreme Court rewrote, with profound social consequence, major constitutional doctrines governing race relations, the administration of criminal justice, and the operation of the political process. The extent and rapidity of the changes raise grave questions concerning the proper role of the Supreme Court in our national development — questions concerning the nature and function of constitutional adjudication.

In these lectures I have tried to describe the main lines of constitutional development under the Warren Court and to analyze (1) the underlying pressures that produced the changes and (2) the long-range institutional consequences in terms of the distribution of governmental power. The unifying theme, if my effort has succeeded, is the strange American paradox which vests in the judicial branch the responsibility for deciding "according to law" major aspects of our most pressing and divisive social, economic, and political questions.

The lectures were written for a general audience of laymen and lawyers at a summer school conducted in Honolulu in 1967 by the Harvard Law School in conjunction with the University of Hawaii. In preparing the manuscript for book publication I have included paragraphs that the limitation of time forced me to omit in oral delivery and have added notes referring the professional reader to the precedents illustrating general observations.

The reader will have to judge for himself how far personal involvement in a number of the cases as Solicitor General of the United States has impaired my ability to review them with academic detachment.

Archibald Cox
November 1967

About the Author

From January 24, 1961, to July 31, 1965, Archibald Cox was Solicitor General of the United States, representing the government in cases before the Supreme Court. From May until October 1973 he served as Special Watergate Prosecutor in the Department of Justice. Except for these periods he has served since 1945 on the faculty of the Harvard Law School, where he is Samuel Williston Professor of Law.

Contents

The Warren Court

1   The Basic Dilemma

POLITICAL STORMS HAVE RAGED around the Supreme Court of the United States almost from the beginning. John Marshall, now universally hailed as our preeminent Chief Justice, was the victim of more vitriolic attacks than Earl Warren almost from the time he ascended the bench in 1801. The difference is that, although the demands for the impeachment of Chief Justice Warren come from a handful of extremists, the plan to impeach Chief Justice Marshall was a plank in the political program of the Jeffersonian Democrats, who held the Presidency and controlled, with large majorities, both houses of Congress. The House of Representatives voted to impeach Marshall's colleague, Samuel Chase, and the Senate acquitted him only because a few Senators ignored party discipline in order to preserve the independence of the judiciary. Had the vote been the reverse, Marshall's impeachment would surely have followed.

The source of these controversies is the peculiar nature of the Supreme Court's business. Count de Tocqueville remarked more than a century ago that hardly a political issue arose in the United States that was not converted into a legal question and taken to the courts for decision. Today de Tocqueville's observation is even closer to the mark; and it applies particularly to the Supreme Court. Part of the docket is unusual only in its difficulty, but the other part—much the more important part—is utterly unlike the usual flow of litigation through the State and lower federal courts. Many of the cases would never come before the judiciary in any other country. Where else would one find a court charged with deciding whether prayers should be said or the Bible read at the start of the day in the school house? Whether Negroes were entitled to equal public accommodations? Or how the seats should be apportioned in a State legislature? To take a quite different example, where else would a court undertake to apportion the waters of a great river system, thus determining the relative opportunities for agricultural and industrial development in vast regions, as our Supreme Court did in apportioning the waters of the Colorado River? In the United States as nowhere else in the world we have developed the extraordinary habit of casting critical aspects of social, economic, political, and philosophical questions in the form of actions at law and suits in equity so that the courts may participate in their disposition.

Since the Court does not always have the last word and may itself shift direction, it is not only inevitable but right that public controversy should be part of the process of ultimate resolution.

One great issue beneath the controversy between Jefferson and Marshall was much like the fundamental question that lies at the bottom of the storm over the Warren Court. What role should the judicial branch play in the government of the American people? Should the Court play an active, creative role in shaping our destiny, equally with the executive and legislative branches? Or should it be characterized by self-restraint, deferring to the legislative branch whenever there is room for policy judgment and leaving new departures to the initiative of others?

Under Marshall the Court staked out an active role in government, building up the power of the federal judiciary and shaping the relation between the Nation and the States according to Marshall's nationalism. *Marbury* v. *Madison*[1] asserted judicial power to issue decrees requiring the Secretary of State to take action contrary to the direct orders of the President, and exercised the authority to declare acts of Congress unconstitutional. The Jeffersonians—the liberals of the early nineteenth century—believed that the Court was too active and should be subordinated to the will of the people. In their view, impeachment implied no wrongdoing; it was simply a mechanism for removing a judge whose views were contrary to the wishes of the electorate.

Defining the Court's role in government also became a major issue early in the present century. Both the Supreme Court and inferior courts used the power to declare laws unconstitutional in order to invalidate much of the modern legislation that we now accept as a normal governmental function—laws on minimum wages and maximum hours, on price regulation, and on labor relations and consumer protection. Most people thought such measures were required by our transformation into a modern industrial and predominantly urban community. Most judges regarded them as dangerous innovations threatening the American way of life. Their judicial activism prevailed until the mid-1930's. It is often associated with the name of Chief Justice Taft.

In reaction, there developed the theory of judicial self-restraint with which the senior generation of lawyers was generally indoctrinated. The theory sprang from the soil of the old Jeffersonian philosophy but was more sophisticated because it allowed room for judicial review in a narrow class of cases. Stated affirmatively, the rationale of judicial self-restraint embraces three propositions:

First, the courts should avoid constitutional issues whenever possible. Such issues should be decided only when raised in ordinary litigation by one who could show that his own constitutional rights were violated and who could not prevail without a constitutional decision.

Second, the courts should not invalidate laws unless they were inconsistent with some specific constitutional prohibition.

Third, wherever there was room for rational difference of opinion upon a question of fact or upon the relative importance of different facts or conflicting interests — one might say, "upon the relative merits of different social policies" — the doctrines of federalism and separation of powers would require the Court to uphold the legislation.

The philosophy of self-restraint came to be associated with the names of Brandeis, Holmes, Learned Hand, and Felix Frankfurter. It was so far dominant within the Supreme Court after 1937 that by the mid-forties it had hardly any critics.

But the issue concerning the proper role of the Supreme Court never lies quiet very long. The appointment of Earl Warren as Chief Justice of the United States marked the beginning of an era of extraordinarily rapid development in our constitutional law during which the Court has broken new ground for the States and other branches of the federal government. Its defenders rightly point out that the Court has spearheaded the progress in civil rights, administration of criminal justice, protection of individual liberty, and the strengthening and extension of political democracy. The critics charge the Court with subordinating law to personal political preferences, and with acting like a legislature or an omnipotent council of not-so-wise wise men instead of a court.

In my view, constitutional adjudication presents an insoluble dilemma. The extraordinary character of the questions put before the Court means that the Court cannot ignore the politi-

cal aspects of its task—the public consequences of its decisions—yet the answer to the question "what substantive result
is best for the country?" is often inconsistent with the responses
obtained by asking "what is the decision according to law?" The
Court may incline to one direction or the other, but no one could
wisely and permanently grasp either horn of the dilemma.

Since the antinomy lies at the heart of constitutional adjudication, I shall repeatedly return to this central theme in the double
effort both to describe the dilemma and to appraise the balance
struck by the Warren Court. The approach of any judge,
however, will be influenced, at least in some degree, by his sense
of the dominant needs of the time and the urgency of their
embodiment into law. Accordingly, this first lecture deals
primarily with the forces pressing upon the Warren Court.

II

The strongest force in current constitutional development is
the demand for racial justice. The judiciary has been more
sensitive to the wrongs of discrimination and segregation than
either the executive or legislative branch of government. The
unanimous decision in the school desegregation cases gave
impetus to the civil rights movement both by discarding the
misguided doctrine of "separate but equal facilities" and by
lighting a beacon of hope for the Negro. The elementary justice
of the resulting expectations created a need for national action
to accomplish a revolution in race relations within the framework of the rule of law, and this need forced reexamination of
the distribution of power within the federal system in relation to
the exercise of responsibility for elections, the legislative powers of Congress, and the relations between State and federal

courts. The problems of racial discrimination in the private sector — in places of public accommodation and in housing, for example — precipitated reexamination of the "State action" doctrine which once rendered the equal protection clause of the Fourteenth Amendment inapplicable to restaurants, hospitals, private schools, and other nongovernmental undertakings. It is worth noting in passing that the problems of the civil rights revolution also affected cases that were apparently unrelated to civil rights. Many purely procedural questions, for instance, were influenced by the realization that in another case they might affect the posture of a Negro in a hostile southern court.

Once loosed, the idea of Equality is not easily cabined. In 1868 the proposal of a constitutional amendment forbidding racial discrimination in voting aroused wide support for a declaration of universal suffrage. Although the declaration was ultimately defeated, it attracted strong support in Congress. Similarly, revitalization of the constitutional prohibitions against racial discrimination in 1954 under *Brown* v. *Board of Education*[2] gave impetus to review of other inequalities in American life. Egalitarianism thus became the second powerful factor shaping current constitutional decisions.

One perceives the force of egalitarianism most clearly in decisions dealing with the processes of government. *Gray* v. *Sanders*,[3] *Wesberry* v. *Sanders*,[4] and *Reynolds* v. *Sims*[5] made it plain that both elections and representation in the legislature must accord voters per capita equality without regard to economic interest or place of residence within the political unit. *Harper* v. *Virginia Board of Elections*[6] invalidated the long-familiar and twice-upheld State laws making payment of the poll tax a prerequisite to voting. The opinion of the Court, written by Justice Douglas, holds that the equal protection clause requires absolute equality for rich and poor in matters pertaining to the franchise: "Wealth, like race, creed, or color, is not germane to one's ability to participate intelligently in the electoral process."[7]

The influence of egalitarianism is also exemplified in decisions concerning the administration of criminal justice. *Griffin* v. *Illinois*[8] held that where a stenographic transcript of the trial is required for full appellate review, a State violates the Fourteenth Amendment by refusing to furnish the transcript to any indigent defendant who alleges serious errors. *Gideon* v. *Wainwright*[9] required the States to supply counsel at public expense to paupers charged with serious crimes. *Douglas* v. *California*[10] extended the latter holding to paupers' appeals to the initial court of review. The relative importance of due process and equal protection in this line of cases is not easily divined, but in *Douglas* v. *California* the theme is plainly that—"where the merits of *the one and only appeal* an indigent has as of right are decided without benefit of counsel . . . an unconstitutional line has been drawn between rich and poor."[11]

The impact of the Court's egalitarianism has been enhanced by the growing belief that government has an affirmative duty to eliminate inequalities and perhaps to provide opportunities for the exercise of other fundamental human rights. The original Bill of Rights was essentially negative. It marked off a world of the spirit in which government should have no jurisdiction; it raised procedural barriers to unwarranted intrusion. It assumed, however, that in this realm the citizen had no claim upon government except to be left alone. Today the same political theory which acknowledges the duty of government to provide jobs, housing, and medical care extends to human rights and imposes an obligation to promote liberty, equality, and dignity. Of course, the recognized political obligation need not become constitutional, and one cannot say with any assurance that the concepts of due process and equal protection have come to require affirmative State action for the benefit of its citizens. Yet the force of the idea of a State with obligations to help its members does seem to have increasing influence in our constitutional law. The idea seems to find expression, for example, in a number of cases involving racial discrimination and in the decisions requiring a State to offset the effects of poverty by providing counsel, transcripts on appeal, and expert witnesses in criminal cases. We may learn more when challenges to *de facto* school segregation come before the Supreme Court.

Concern for personal liberty and privacy against governmental intrusions is the fourth major element in the recent development of constitutional law. The Framers consciously committed this function to the judiciary, but its flowering was reserved for an age in which the increasing interdependence and complexity of all parts of human society have multiplied and magnified governmental activities. The wide spread of public regulation increases the occasions on which government collides with personal liberty. The collisions warn of the necessity for marking off a private spiritual area from which government should be excluded. The young men and women growing up at a time when government is playing the largest role in society show the most concern with defense of the individual in the realm of the spirit. The abuses of McCarthyism in the early 1950's, which shocked the intellectual community, undoubtedly enhanced awareness of the threats to liberty inherent in fears of Communist subversion and aggression.

All these political forces, in an era characterized by continuing social and intellectual revolt against traditional restraints, have helped to produce strongly libertarian decisions on a variety of issues ranging from marital privacy to political demonstrations. The revolution in the law of obscenity and the invalidation of State loyalty oaths and other statutes aimed at barring so-called "subversives" from public employment will serve as examples.

The frequency with which the Court invalidated the acts of State legislatures interfering with civil liberties — and its occasional invalidation of Congressional action — posed a theoretical problem with wider ramifications. Years before, the Jeffersonians had argued that judicial review of legislative action violated the principle that the people should rule. In the twentieth century their descendants prevailed at least to the extent of establishing such doctrines as (1) that the courts should avoid substituting the judges' views of policy for those of the legislature under the guise of interpreting broad phrases like "due process" and "equal protection of the law"; (2) that the courts should presume the existence of facts which would justify the challenged action if they could rationally be supposed to exist; and (3) that the courts should uphold the acts of the legislature whenever a rational man might have reached the legislature's conclusion. The present Court was unwilling to follow this course in dealing with personal rights ranging from speech and association to voting and birth control. It thus became necessary to explain why the doctrine of legislative supremacy which obtains in reviewing the regulation of property and business conduct does not apply to personal liberties.

The most satisfying reconciliation developed along these lines: Where the channels of debate and representative self-government are open, it is fair to say to one claiming under the due process clause that a law is so unjust as to be unconstitutional, "You must seek correction through the political process, for the judiciary to intervene would be a denial of self-government." This is no answer, however, when the statute under attack closes the political process to particular ideas or particular groups, or otherwise distorts its operation. Then the correction must come from outside and no violence is done to the principles of representative government if the Court supplies the remedy. The latter reasoning applies to both speech and other political liberties such as freedom of association.

In recent years the Court has been increasingly explicit about the link between the preferred position accorded First Amendment freedoms and the operation of representative self-government. In *New York Times Co.* v. *Sullivan*[12] and subsequent cases it adopted Dr. Alexander Meiklejohn's theory that whereas other provisions of the Bill of Rights place limits upon powers granted to the government in favor of the citizen, the guarantees of freedom of speech and the press are really reserved powers totally withheld from the government by the people, who are the ultimate rulers. The rationale expands and solidifies the protection of free speech and relates it to the operation of popular self-government.

Rationalizing the preferred position of speech and other political liberties upon these grounds naturally leads to the conclusion that the Court has a wider responsibility for the open and democratic operation of our political system. The conscious sense of this responsibility is a striking characteristic distinguishing the present Court from all its predecessors. In the area of speech the Court is preserving and extending an inherited tradition. There the most striking feature is the clarity of the Court's vision of a society characterized by endless self-renewal—a process which depends upon tolerance of the small bands of "way out" heretics seeking to overturn the established order, for history reveals that some among the extremists initiate the greatest progress in human institutions.

The Court broke new ground when it exercised constitutional control over the apportionment of representatives and voting qualifications. The decisions carried forward the basic view that the Court has special responsibility for the democratic integrity of political processes but they also raised with excruciating intensity the central dilemma of constitutional adjudication.

By stressing the political side of the Court's concern for civil liberties I do not mean to minimize the deeply humanitarian impulse evident in those decisions—an impulse most evident in its extraordinary reforms in criminal procedure. Despite much history and earlier precedents sustaining it, a constitutional stop has been put to the inexcusable wrong wrought by many States in trying men for serious crimes without the aid of counsel because they were too poor to retain an attorney.[13] That simple safeguard has stimulated countless local measures correcting other injustices in criminal procedure. No longer may a State court follow the prevailing and apparently well-settled practice of allowing the police to use evidence obtained by an unlawful arrest or by entering a house without a warrant, in order to obtain a conviction.[14] The law of confessions has been rewritten.[15] A start has been made upon developing standards governing the admission and exclusion of evidence obtained by wire-tapping and other forms of electronic surveillance.[16] One could add other, scarcely less important examples. Never has there been such thoroughgoing reform of our rules of criminal procedure within so short a space of time.

The criminal cases suggest a final element operating on the current development of constitutional law. Modern psychology has raised doubts concerning freedom of the will that raise skepticism of the very notion of crime. Sociologists have cast doubt upon the efficacy of punishment and deterrence in the face of the social, economic, and psychological causes of criminal conduct. When an issue is nicely balanced between the interests of the public and the claims of individual liberty, the substitution of such doubts for once-accepted verities may be enough to tip the scales against the prosecution.

If this is true in criminal procedure, may not similar forces be partly responsible for the turmoil in other areas of constitutional law? We live in a time of intellectual as well as economic and political upheaval. While the physical scientists are rewriting Newton's laws and the social scientists changing our understanding of man—while the actual condition of man is revolutionized—judges will inevitably be stimulated to reexamine the law's own presuppositions. One wonders, indeed, whether the gulf between the Supreme Court and the Congress is not partly a reflection of the closer kinship the justices have with the intellectual community.

III

If one judges solely by the immediate legal results of Supreme Court decisions, the current era must be called a time of extraordinary creativity and progress. True, there is room to argue that sentimentality has replaced judgment in individual cases, or that dogma has been run into the ground at the expense of the fundamental interests the Court was seeking to secure. Perhaps the progress has gone too far too fast in some areas—possibly in the reform of criminal procedure. But after such qualifications are noted, surely there would be general and enthusiastic praise for the main lines of development—if laid down by a bevy of Platonic guardians instead of a court. There can be very few who would wish to revive the caste system under the pretense of "separate but equal"; to restore rural domination of State legislatures by systematic malapportionment; or to revive trials without the aid of counsel or through the psychological extortion of confessions.

The problem is more complex for those who think partly in institutional terms and believe that in the long run human events may be profoundly influenced by the allocation of power among governmental agencies and by the way in which the judiciary exercises its share of power—more complex not because they are any less enthusiastic over the substantive progress but because it has been accompanied by major institutional changes whose long-range consequences are difficult to measure and which the present Court sometimes seems to brush aside without careful consideration in its enthusiasm for immediate progress. It is this conflict between substantive progress and institutional needs that creates the basic dilemma of constitutional adjudication.

IV

One institutional change is the expansion of federal judicial power at the expense of the States.

The trend is most apparent in the shift of ultimate responsibility for rules governing the administration of criminal justice. So long as the due process clause condemned only procedure that shocked a sense of fundamental fairness, State law governed most aspects of criminal investigation and procedure, and the Supreme Court rarely intervened. Now that due process has been held to incorporate virtually all the guarantees of the Bill of Rights, the final word upon many of the details of State trials has been transferred not only to the Supreme Court of the United States but also to the inferior federal courts, which have jurisdiction to review federal constitutional claims, after conviction, upon application for habeas corpus.

Similarly, parts of the law of libel are being nationalized. The

New York Times case[17] created a First Amendment privilege to publish matter which turns out to be defamatory of a public official provided that the publisher was neither aware of the falsehood nor recklessly indifferent to the truth. Later the privilege was extended to all reports about figures in whose character or activities the public feels an interest.[18] Much the same rule is also applied to defamation in the course of labor disputes, albeit as an acknowledged judicial creation rather than as constitutional law.[19] This means that the Supreme Court rather than the State courts will have the last word upon much of the law of libel.

For a third illustration consider the enlargement of the role of the federal judiciary implicit in the decisions rendering State voting laws and State apportionment of legislative representatives subject to scrutiny under the equal protection clause.

The enlargement of federal judicial power has been paralleled by the expansion of the powers of Congress—also at the expense of the States. The best example is the interpretation of the long-forgotten Section 5 of the Fourteenth Amendment, which grants Congress the power "to enforce" the equal protection and due process clauses "by appropriate legislation." In 1883, in the *Civil Rights Cases*,[20] the Court declared that the power conferred by Section 5 was limited to correcting the effect of State laws enacted in violation of the Fourteenth Amendment, because any broader interpretation would give Congress authority over the "whole domain of rights appertaining to life, liberty and property, defining them and providing for their vindication" and this "would be to make Congress take the place of the State legislatures and to supersede them." In 1966 *Katzenbach* v. *Morgan*[21] and *United States* v. *Guest*[22] swept the limitation aside, holding that Congress may enact any legislation which it deems appropriate to facilitate the exercise of Fourteenth Amendment rights, and that such legislation may be directed to the interfering activities of individuals as well as the States. The potential of these decisions is illustrated by the fact that they would logically sustain such diverse federal statutes as a code of criminal procedure applicable to State trials and a federal ban upon racial discrimination in the sale or leasing of private housing.

Although the Warren Court has expanded federal judicial power at the expense of the States, its history has been relatively free from the fundamental conflicts between the judicial and legislative branches that marred the constitutional history of the first third of the present century. The Court is not popular in Congress. There has been outspoken criticism and even efforts to nullify its decisions. Acts of Congress and an even larger number of State laws and municipal ordinances have been held unconstitutional. Still, one has the sense that the decisions do not thwart representative democracy in quite the same way as the older cases invalidating the income tax, consumer protection, price regulation, and laws on labor relations and minimum wages. Part of the explanation may be that the present Court is moving with the current whereas the Taft Court sought to reverse it, but there are three other plausible explanations:

(1) The Court's most creative role has been played either in areas which have always been the special prerogative of the judiciary, such as criminal procedure and libel, or else in areas which the legislative branch has neglected, such as school desegregation and reapportionment.

(2) The legislative measures invalidated by the Warren Court were rarely based upon careful study of social and economic needs of the community, and, except in the case of massive resistance to desegregation, were rarely supported by much long-range popular sentiment.

(3) The Court has been noticeably careful to avoid square conflicts, if it can, even in the area of the First Amendment. In the rather numerous cases in which demonstrators have challenged arrests and convictions for disturbing the peace or similar offenses upon the ground of freedom of speech or assembly, the Court has seldom held that the defendants were, in truth, exercising a constitutional right beyond local regulation. Rather, it has set the convictions aside upon such grounds as that the statute was unconstitutionally vague because a man could not tell exactly what conduct was prohibited;[23] or was so broad as to include other conduct which was constitutionally privileged; or left so much discretion to petty officials as to create risks of administrative abuse and indicate that the legislature has not faced up to the hard and specific choice between whatever interests were served by the regulation and the values of expression.[24] A similar note runs through some of the cases voiding convictions for contempt of Congress and even of State legislatures: the primary effort has been to make the investigating committees comply with their own rules and the rules of Congress and to force Congress as a whole to face the civil liberties issues raised by committees investigating "un-American activities" and internal security.[25]

The Warren Court has been quick to slough off the restraints its predecessors erected to limit the occasions for deciding whether and when the Court will adjudicate constitutional issues. The precepts of wise constitutional adjudication that were taught law students in the 1930's counseled postponement and avoidance. Occasionally, in the normal course of adjudicating lawsuits, the Court might be forced to decide whether the governing law was the statute or the Constitution, but such interference with the work of a coordinate branch of the federal government or a sovereign State was thought to be justifiable only in cases of absolute necessity. The party attacking the statute had to show its unconstitutionality as applied to him; the courts would not listen to the claim that it was unconstitutional applied to another. The plaintiff must demonstrate his standing by showing that he was injured by the alleged unconstitutional statute in a way that marked him out from the generality of citizens. Equity would not enjoin the enforcement of an allegedly unconstitutional statute where the unconstitutionality could be raised as a defense in a criminal prosecution, save in the most exceptional conditions. The constitutional battles of the 1930's were often fought on these procedural grounds. Those seeking to sustain new governmental activities, both regulatory and otherwise, could rest satisfied with blocking judicial intervention.

Today, the attitude is changed, and the rules of judicial self-restraint that looked to the avoidance of constitutional rulings have been eroded in opinions strongly suggesting that the present Court believes it has a responsibility to make its influence felt in support or check of other branches of government, or in innovation, even though not coerced by the necessities of litigation. Two examples may be helpful.

(1) When Ollie McClung filed suit to enjoin the enforcement of the 1964 equal-public-accommodations law as unconstitutional if applied to his barbecue restaurant in Birmingham, Alabama, the Department of Justice, never having even heard of Ollie's barbecue, made the conventional objection that equity would not enjoin the enforcement of a statute where the claim of unconstitutionality can be raised as a defense in the event that proceedings are ever brought against the plaintiff. The district court granted the injunction. The Department raised the point again in the Supreme Court, even though confident that the Act was constitutional, partly because the point was jurisdictional

and partly because the government had a long-range interest in avoiding a precedent that would open the door to litigation at the time and place, and in the case, chosen by anyone wishing to attack the constitutionality of novel legislation. It seems to me, even when I try to discount for my bias as the advocate, that the objection surely would have been sustained unanimously during the 1930's. In 1964 the Court unanimously rejected it.[26] So hostile was the questioning at oral argument that I was forced to retreat to the suggestion that the government would welcome a ruling on the merits if only the opinion might contain a dictum warning district courts not to repeat the error. The Court followed the suggestion and upheld the Act on the merits.

The change in the Court's attitude between the 1930's and the 1960's can be technically explained by the development of the declaratory judgment, which was not available in the federal courts during the 1930's and which Justice Brandeis, the chief architect of procedural self-restraints, regarded as unconstitutional. The real explanation runs deeper; the Court was anxious to validate the Civil Rights Act of 1964 because it believed that a prompt constitutional decision would be in the public interest, even though not impelled by the necessities of litigation, whereas a postponement of decision might create uncertainty. In a later case enjoining criminal prosecutions under a State law alleged to interfere with political liberties, the opinion candidly stated that one of the reasons for intervening was that otherwise the existence of the statute and risks of prosecution might deter the exercise of constitutional rights by persons unwilling to risk prosecution.[27] Although the decision itself is only a modest extension, this particular reason seems to assert that, at least to some extent, the Court should act as if it had a roving commission to check other branches of government which may be about to violate the Constitution.

(2) The same theme appears in cases relaxing the requirements of standing. As early as 1940, in *Thornhill* v. *Alabama,* a
defendant convicted under a State law prohibiting all picketing
was allowed to challenge the statute on its face without showing
that his kind of picketing was constitutionally protected, because the "existence of such a statute . . . results in a continuous
and pervasive restraint on all freedom of discussion that might
reasonably be regarded as within its purview."[28] Later cases,
allowing a litigant none of whose own constitutional rights have
been invaded to set up the rights of others, give as one of the
reasons that otherwise the constitutional challenge might not be
raised.[29] The emphasis now is on the Court's function as protector of a public interest in the enforcement of constitutional
limitations. It used to be on the need to avoid conflict with other
branches of government equally bound by the Constitution and
equally able to discharge the obligation.

The issue may be put to its sharpest test in cases challenging
the financial assistance rendered to parochial schools under
federal aid-to-education as a violation of the First Amendment's
prohibition against enactment of a law respecting an establishment of religion. A federal taxpayer has no standing to challenge
the constitutionality of expenditures from general funds. There
are no individuals who can show that the federal grants do them
some material harm or restrain their freedom in ways distinct
from the injury done to all other members of the community.
Any wrong suffered by members of other faiths is not the kind of
injury ordinarily subject to judicial redress. If those rules are
applied, there may never be a Supreme Court ruling upon the
constitutionality of the grants, just as there probably can be
none (albeit for a different reason) upon whether fighting a war
in Viet Nam without a declaration of war by Congress violates
the Constitution.[30]

But the rules have not always been followed strictly. Any voter may challenge the constitutionality of the apportionment of representatives in the legislature even though the substantial wrong is not to him but to the whole underrepresented part of the body politic. In the school prayer and Bible-reading cases, the Court allowed any parent to challenge the practice who had children in the schools. It would be no great extension of the precedents to say that members of other religious sects or antireligious faiths suffer legally cognizable disadvantage through government aid to parochial schools.

Beneath these technical arguments lies the more nearly fundamental question: how broad a commission should the Supreme Court assume to police the interpretation of the Constitution by other branches of government? The philosophical battle over federal aid to parochial schools proved scarcely less divisive than other religious controversies. It caused serious delay in providing essential funds for the improvement of primary and secondary education. Eventually a legislative accommodation was reached which apparently proved acceptable to the great bulk of the people. If its implementation caused anyone the kind of harm for which judicial remedies are customarily available when the harm is inflicted illegally, then the judiciary should perform its customary duty of deciding whether the infliction was illegal; but when there is no harm of that nature — or at best borderline harm — one is free to ask whether anything is gained by substituting the intellectual decision of a majority of nine justices for the more pragmatic political accommodation of the elected representatives of the people. Both can fairly be said to be interpreting the First Amendment. Neither of the possible conclusions can be said to be commanded by the words, "Congress shall make no law respecting an establishment of religion."

The precepts restricting the occasions for constitutional

adjudication are major elements in the distinction between determination by a Council of Wise Men and decision by a court. No less important is the precept that the Court is to decide not by what is good, or just, or wise, but according to law, according to a continuity of principle found in the words of the Constitution, judicial precedents, traditional understanding and like sources of law. It is in these terms that there is the greatest professional criticism of the present Court. The wholesale discard of precedent and the readiness to overturn, by bare majority, doctrines reaffirmed by the Court just prior to the last change in its membership do no service to the idea of law as something distinct from politics and the arbitrary preferences of individuals. The majority has been notably unsuccessful in rationalizing new departures under the equal protection clause, and, when cynically minded, one wonders whether it has made much effort. Occasionally decisions seem to turn on intuitive judgments of right and wrong rather than the impartial application of principle. Witness the current confusion in the law of obscenity.

Ability to rationalize a constitutional judgment in terms of principles referable to accepted sources of law is an essential, major element of constitutional adjudication. It is one of the ultimate sources of the power of the Court — including the power to gain acceptance for the occasional great leaps forward which lack such justification. Constitutional government must operate by consent of the governed. Court decrees draw no authority from the participation of the people. Their power to command consent depends upon more than habit or even the deserved prestige of the justices. It comes, to an important degree, from the continuing force of the rule of law — from the belief that the major influence in judicial decisions is not fiat but principles which bind the judges as well as the litigants and which apply consistently among all men today, and also yesterday and tomorrow. I cannot prove these points, but they are the faith to which we lawyers are dedicated.

This faith represents only one branch of the basic dilemma of constitutional adjudication. In times of economic, social, and even moral upheaval the danger of exaggerating the importance of certainty and stability as elements of law is probably greater than the risk of valuing it too lightly. There is also the danger that fascination with the lawyer's art may divert us from the human goals of the enterprise. Legal logic has no value for its own sake. Law is a human instrument designed to meet men's needs. The ultimate goals of the law are no different from those of a Council of Wise Men. The question is, how much and how fast can a court pursue what it sees as the goals of society without impairing the long run usefulness of judge-made law in contributing to their achievement.

Judge Learned Hand, in a tribute to Cardozo, described this antinomy at the basis of a judge's work: "His authority and immunity depend upon the assumption that he speaks with the mouth of others: the momentum of his utterances must be greater than any which his personal reputation and character can command, if it is to do the work assigned to it—if it is to stand against the passionate resentments arising out of the interests he must frustrate . . . Yet the customary law of English-speaking people stands as a structure indubitably made by the hands of generations of judges . . . A judge must manage to escape both horns of this dilemma: he must preserve his authority by cloaking himself in the majesty of an over-shadowing past; but he must discover some composition with the dominant needs of his times."[31]

The dilemma is insoluble. There is no rule by which a judge may know where to place the emphasis, nor any scale by which the contemporary critic can measure the balance struck. The gains of decisions advancing social justice are evident when they are rendered; any costs in erosion of the power of law to command consent are postponed until the loss accumulates. Granting the mystery, there will be few who, if they could relive recent history, would choose to exchange closer attention to conventional legal doctrines for the great strides taken under the leadership of the Warren Court in civil rights, the strengthening of democratic self-government, and the administration of criminal justice. The question to keep before us is whether a better partial reconciliation might not sometimes be achieved by more attention to professional method. For the function of the whole elaborate structure of legal reasoning is to ease the dilemma by preserving the power of judge-made law to command consent while at the same time changing it to serve the new and newly felt needs of the community and the demands of individual justice.

2 Civil Rights: Judicial Innovation

THE CONSTITUTIONAL LITIGATION of any era reflects the problems and divisions in the contemporary society. No other force operating in the second half of the twentieth century approaches in importance the pressures generated by the coming of age of the peoples of Asia and Africa. Cast in domestic terms the issue was—and is—between better realization of the promise of the Declaration of Independence, that all men are created equal, and adherence to ways of life rooted in the habits of our people, North as well as South, since before the signing of the Declaration.

The constitutional issues precipitated by the civil rights movement thus became the focal point of the work of the Warren Court. On the one hand, settled rules of constitutional law, including the accepted distribution of governmental power between States and Nation, did little to facilitate and much to obstruct the civil rights movement. On the other hand, problems of school desegregation, "sit-in" litigation, and the constitutionality of civil rights legislation could not be decided wisely—nor can the process of constitutional adjudication be understood—without taking account of the fact that the civil rights movement required that the Court preside over parts of a social and political revolution seeking accomplishment within the frame of constitutionalism, if possible, yet ready if necessary to burst the bonds of law. The resulting tension strained the process of constitutional adjudication, and profoundly influenced the recent course of our constitutional history.

I

The legal font was *Brown* v. *Board of Education*.[1] The essence of that oft-told tale also reveals a good deal about the process of deciding constitutional questions. The issue was whether a State which maintained separate schools for white and Negro children thereby denied Negro children "equal protection of the law" in violation of the Fourteenth Amendment. In 1896 the Supreme Court itself had decided that compulsory segregation on railway trains did not violate the equal protection clause, provided that the separate facilities furnished to each race were actually equal. The rule spread into every aspect of life in the South and, to a degree, into other regions. Later, a few qualifications developed, but *Plessy* v. *Ferguson*[2] was still authoritative when *Brown* v. *Board of Education* came before the Court. The Court rejected the established doctrine and held that racial segregation in public schools violated the Fourteenth Amendment's guarantee of "equal protection of the law."

To have followed precedent would have served one important aspect of law. Our system of constitutional adjudication depends upon a vast reservoir of respect for law and courts. Law can serve as both the government's substitute for force and the citizen's protector of freedom against the government (whose force is overwhelming) only so long as law commands a large degree of voluntary acceptance. The acceptance of constitutional decisions — the habit of compliance or force of legitimacy, if you prefer — seems to rest, in turn, at least partly upon the understanding that what the judge decides is not simply his personal notion of what is desirable but the application of rules that apply to all men equally, yesterday, today, and tomorrow.

One of the lessons of *Brown* v. *Board of Education* is that there are limits to the power of even the Supreme Court to command assent. The failure to follow *Plessy* v. *Ferguson* damaged the principle of legitimacy because men disappointed by the new decision were able to excuse disobedience by saying, "The desegregation ruling is not law, but the dictate of nine men. In time, with nine different men, the Court will return to its earlier decisions." The strain thus put upon the Court's position, in terms of the capacity to do one of the major jobs assigned to law, did not pass unobserved in subsequent litigation.

I am far from suggesting that the decision in the school desegregation cases was wrong even in the most technical sense. To have adhered to the doctrine of "separate but equal" would have ignored not only the revolution sweeping the world but the moral sense of civilization. Law must be binding even upon the highest court, but it must also meet the needs of men and match their ethical sensibilities. The dilemma lies at the root of Anglo-American jurisprudence. There have always been occasions when the courts, to shape the law to these objectives, have had to pay the price of revealing that judges sometimes make law to suit the occasion. Nor should we forget that not to pay that price may even defeat the object of obtaining voluntary compliance, because law, to command consent, must deserve it.

The *Brown* case also illustrates another aspect of constitutional adjudication. Although the justices have differed sharply upon the propriety of using the bench as a "bully pulpit," one suspects that the course of decision is sometimes influenced, in great cases, by the realization that the influence of the Supreme

Court's opinions goes far beyond the formal limits of its decrees. The Court is often the voice of the national conscience. The justices shape, as well as express, our national ideals. *Brown* v. *Board of Education* restated the spirit of America and lighted a beacon of hope for Negroes at a time when other governmental voices were silent. To make the Court's abstract constitutional declaration a reality has required the support of the legislative branch and will require still more vigorous executive action, but no one can suppose that those would have been forthcoming in the 1960's but for the "nonjudicial power" of the Court. Awareness of this function is a force pressing against mere adherence to existing law.

II

In terms of legal principle there was no problem in extending *Brown's* promise of racial equality throughout the realm of official action. Any thought that only schools were affected was soon dissipated by a series of cases holding that the guarantee of equal protection condemns any form of affirmative, hostile discrimination or segregation by governmental activity upon grounds of race or color. The difficulties — still unresolved — lay, and lie, in the field of private action. (Here and elsewhere I use the word "private" in contrast with "official" or "governmental." Most of the private action with which we shall be dealing is public in the sense that it is out-in-the-open and has public consequences.)

As late as 1960 no constitutional principle seemed better settled than that the Fourteenth Amendment does not reach private action. The guarantee of equal protection is addressed, in terms, only to States. The amendment speaks, in terms, only of equal protection *of the laws:*

> No State shall ... deny to any person ... equal protection of the laws.

Beginning in the 1880's a series of Supreme Court decisions consistently held, first, that only a State or a person acting under color of State authority can violate the Fourteenth Amendment; and, second, that the power of Congress to enforce the amendment by appropriate legislation extends only to State violations. In 1883, in the *Civil Rights Cases*,[3] the Court unanimously invalidated an equal-public-accommodations law enacted by Congress to enforce the Fourteenth Amendment. A third point, though never adjudicated, was taken for granted: the Fourteenth Amendment imposes no affirmative duties upon the States to bring about racial equality; they are merely required to refrain from imposing special burdens or making invidious distinctions in withholding from one class the benefits or protection accorded to another.

It needs no argument to show that while these doctrines stood, the promise of human equality for Negroes could not be realized within the frame of law. The brand of inferior caste was —and is—imposed by segregation or discrimination in hotels, theaters, restaurants, and other places of public accommodation, by discrimination in employment, and by discrimination and segregation in the sale or rental of housing. The mere prevention of further official discrimination leaves other, built-in inequalities untouched—for example, *de facto* school segregation. The States have ample power to remedy the wrongs but no one could suppose that each of the fifty States would enact the necessary legislation. National action was required to correct the wrongs; yet the pressures for national action collided with the earlier doctrines. The pressure points, and therefore the putative lines of development, after *Brown* v. *Board of Education* corresponded to the propositions just stated:

First, the Court might abandon the doctrine that the Fourteenth Amendment applies only to State action and, by judicial process alone, require private activities of public consequence to be conducted in accordance with the same standards of equality applicable to the States. In other words, the Court might hold that the Fourteenth Amendment itself operates, without aid of legislation, to prohibit private, racial discrimination in nongovernmental sectors of society such as housing, employment, privately endowed universities, and places of public accommodation.

Second, the Congress might be persuaded to enact legislation forbidding private racial discrimination, and the Court might be induced to uphold the enactment either under the commerce clause or by virtue of an expanded concept of the power of Congress "to enforce" the equal protection clause of the Fourteenth Amendment "by appropriate legislation."

Change under either head would require modification or abandonment of the traditional constitutional distinction between State and private action. In the one case the new restriction upon a wide range of conduct would be imposed by judicial reinterpretation of the Constitution. In the other the revision would have the support of legislation by elected representatives of the people.

III

Before we come to the cases it is worth noting that the seemingly simple dichotomy between State action and private action becomes remarkably elusive when one seeks to apply it to modern institutions. The activities of government are vastly expanded, with the result that both government and private enterprises are often engaged in the same activities—utilities, education, and housing may be the best examples. Frequently the government chooses to provide for public needs by furnishing private institutions with the necessary funds and establishing the substantive standards and administrative supervision necessary to ensure that the public purposes will be fulfilled. Is the action of Harvard University private action or State action for the purposes of the Fourteenth Amendment? A large percentage of its annual expenditures comes from government funds, both for research and education. Hospitals built or improved by charitable corporations under the Hill-Burton Act are a still better example, for they are largely financed with government funds and integrated into State plans for the public provision of hospital care even though the management is nongovernmental.

To jump to a very different field, consider the mixture of private organization and governmental support that enters into the activities of a labor union. Initially a voluntary association and always partly dependent upon its economic power, the labor union, once chosen by a majority, has a status as exclusive bargaining representative of the employees that is conferred by law; and it is by law that the union's undertakings govern the working conditions, and loose and bind the obligations, of employees in the bargaining unit, without their individual consent. Inasmuch as the status and power of a union are thus derived partly from government, should one say that the union's action is or is not governmental action for the purposes of the Fifth or Fourteenth Amendments? Very similar questions suggest themselves with respect to the New York Stock Exchange and the bar associations to which one is required by law to belong in order to practice his profession.

Regulation may also mean involvement. A government that supervises many details of an enterprise can hardly disclaim all responsibility for those which it could equally well regulate but chooses to leave untouched. Indeed, the forms of involvement are as varied as human undertakings. Even a private seminary for young ladies which receives no public grants is dependent upon substantial State support in the form of tax exemptions for its own property, charitable deductions for givers in computing their income tax, the exemption from the rule against perpetuities (an exemption which commits endowment to the operation of such a school through future generations), the police protection which evicts trespassers, and so forth. For a last example, consider the restaurant located in the municipal parking facility in Wilmington, Delaware. The facility was a tax-exempt building which was constructed with public funds and the aid of the power of eminent domain, which flew the Delaware flag, and which was operated as a public building except for the store-front leases. Yet the restaurant was privately owned and operated. It was in this case that the Court, mindful of these complications, observed that the question whether private conduct violates the equal protection clause depended upon whether "to some significant extent the State in any of its manifestations has been found to have become involved in it."[4]

One of the major problems of constitutional law is to formulate and express a judgment upon what degree of State involvement is "significant" for the purposes of the Fourteenth Amendment. Another is to avoid losing sight of the basic issues concerning the character of our society among all the details that may or may not show State involvement.

IV

The cases arising out of the sit-in demonstrations of the late fifties and early sixties posed the issue in its sharpest form, and they are thus unusually revealing about both the special problem of State action and the general nature of constitutional adjudication. Negroes, sometimes accompanied by white sympathizers, entered restaurants or lunch counters that refused to serve food to Negroes or practiced segregation. They stayed despite the operator's refusal of service and request to leave his premises. Arrest, trial, and conviction usually followed, with criminal trespass the charge. In due course the Supreme Court was asked to hold that the States where these incidents occurred had denied the Negroes equal protection of the law.

The issue would have been easy for a Council of Wise Men. Racial discrimination in places of public accommodation ought to be abolished. A decision sustaining the convictions of the sit-in demonstrators might injure the entire civil rights movement; it would surely have impaired Negroes' confidence in the legal order. Omniscient and omnipotent Platonic guardians would have quickly voided the convictions.

For a court — even a court of constitutional law — the problem was harder. If adjudication ought normally to be rooted in a continuous community of principle found in the words of the Constitution, in judicial precedents, constitutional practice, and like sources of law — not for the sake of legal logic but because the observance of this limitation is necessary to the viability of a constitutionalism based upon judicial review — then the State prosecutors had much the better of the argument. This was so not because the established law favored racial discrimination but because nongovernmental discrimination had never been treated as the action of a State for the purposes of the Fourteenth Amendment.

Perhaps the precedents could have been gotten over as in the school desegregation cases, but there were other obstacles to ruling that prosecution for trespassing at a segregated lunch counter violates the Fourteenth Amendment. The most serious was the difficulty of devising a rule favorable to the demonstrators which the courts could apply in the future with logical consistency. Each of the various theories offered is worth examining in detail because they are still vital forces in constitutional law.

One theory was that arrest, prosecution, and conviction of crime is enough State action to bring the amendment into play. The States replied that what the Fourteenth Amendment prohibits is not State action but State discrimination, and that their action was truly color-blind since they would deal in like fashion with anyone and everyone who invaded private property without the owner's consent. The rejoinder was that the Supreme Court in *Shelley* v. *Kraemer,* reversing a State court decree that had enforced a restrictive racial covenant written by private agreement, had said: "... these are cases in which the States have made available to such individuals the full coercive power of government to deny to petitioners, on the grounds of race or color, the enjoyment of property rights ... Nor is the Amendment ineffective simply because the particular pattern of discrimination, which the State enforced, was defined initially by the terms of a private agreement."[5] From this precedent it was argued that the Fourteenth Amendment is violated whenever a State puts the power of the police or the judiciary behind a private decision to engage in racial discrimination.

Yet the argument seems to prove too much. Civilized individual liberty depends upon the availability of legal sanctions against aggression. Private choice is either empty or dangerous to society if its effective exercise depends upon private armies and willingness to use them against aggression.

Thus it avails a man little to be told that he may select the neighbors whom he will invite to his swimming pool unless he may call upon the police to exclude the uninvited. Immoral as his choice to exclude a Negro or a Japanese neighbor may be, the Constitution could hardly be supposed to forbid it. There are patent differences between racial discrimination at a public restaurant and a private swimming pool, but the line cannot be drawn in terms of official sanctions for private discrimination, because a prosecution for criminal trespass would involve just as much State action in the one case as the other. Nor is it easy to see how any other differentiation could be justified in terms of the Fourteenth Amendment, which, when it applies, condemns not some, but all, discrimination.

In separate opinions in early sit-in cases Justice Douglas offered a second rationale.[6] One who offers a public service, he said — one who follows a public calling — is performing a function of the State; he is therefore a State instrumentality and his acts are acts of government. The argument derives from the dissenting opinion of the first Justice Harlan in the *Civil Rights Cases,* but I must confess that neither its age nor modern restatement aids my understanding. One cannot say, from observation of the facts, that serving food and drink is the kind of activity in which government engages, as he might possibly say about parks or even schools if it were relevant. The notion seems to equate such words as "public calling" with "government function" and "government instrumentality," largely by confusing the several meanings of "public" and certainly without articulating the reasons for the equation. *A priori* it is possible to treat any enterprise which has significant public consequences as if it were the government for the purposes of the Fourteenth Amendment, but before embracing the proposition one ought to acknowledge that it has no roots in our constitutional history, and the underlying question of policy ought to be examined. In our complex interrelated society, acceptance of Justice Douglas' view would pretty much eliminate any difference between State action and private decision for the purposes of the Fourteenth Amendment. We shall consider in a moment whether that would be a wise constitutional development.

A third potential avenue reaching much the same result would be to reason that the obligations of the State under the equal protection clause extend to taking affirmative steps to prevent invidious discrimination in places of public accommodation. In *Terry* v. *Adams*[7] four justices took the view that Texas had a duty to prevent the Jaybird Club, which dominated the Democratic primaries in a certain county, from discriminating against Negro voting on grounds of race or color. In *Marsh* v. *Alabama*,[8] the Court apparently held that a State which permits a business corporation to establish a population center on private property with all other characteristics of a town has an obligation not to permit it to deny freedom of speech and religion. In the *Wilmington Parking Authority* case,[9] a case mentioned earlier, Justice Clark said: "But no State may effectively abdicate its responsibilities by either ignoring them or by merely failing to discharge them whatever the motive may be . . . *By its inaction*, the Authority, and through it the State, has not only made itself a party to the refusal of service, but has elected to place its power, property and prestige behind the admitted discrimination."[10] (Emphasis supplied.)

The sense that government has affirmative responsibilities for human rights and especially for the elimination of inequalities, whether racial or otherwise, is one of the dominant forces in current constitutional development. By habit we usually think of constitutional limitations as restrictions upon what government can do. They were imposed to protect the States against the national government and the individual against governmental aggression. Contemporary society accepts the political principle that the modern State owes its citizens various obligations — a growing economy, jobs, education, medical care, old-age assistance and so forth. That the principle has been extended to human rights is hardly surprising. Since human rights are secured by the Constitution, it would also be natural to import that part of the political principle into constitutional law. This may well be one of the undercurrents explaining the decisions requiring States to supply indigents with free transcripts of the evidence and with counsel on appeal from criminal convictions in order to eliminate the inequality they would otherwise suffer in comparison with defendants of greater means.[11]

Although the sense that the government has an affirmative obligation to promote equality is plainly influential in cases of racial discrimination, that idea, standing alone, furnishes no rule of decision adequate for evolving a coherent body of law. Is it the State's duty to prohibit discrimination wherever the State has power to regulate? Since there are few limits upon that power, a rule which brought the Fourteenth Amendment into play wherever the State could act would reach beyond lunch counters to all retail sales and service establishments, to doctors, lawyers, and a host of others.

The suggested principle was open-ended in still another respect. How could a court conclude that discrimination at lunch counters violated the Fourteenth Amendment without going on to rule that the amendment is also violated by discrimination in employment, in admitting pupils to private schools and colleges, and in the sale and rental of housing? It would immeasurably advance the cause of human justice to have on the statute books open housing laws, fair employment practices acts, and like legislation; but it would be amazing to find that all the hard legislative fights were unnecessary and the will of the people is irrelevant because the legal requirements were long ago written into the Fourteenth Amendment.

So long as one focuses on racial discrimination and dwells upon the objective without concern for the route by which it is achieved, there is much that is appealing about the total elimination of the requirement of State action and the subjection of anyone whose activities have public aspects to the duties imposed upon the State. However, if the traditional distinction is to be abandoned in that respect, then it must also be obliterated in applying other restrictions that the Fourteenth Amendment imposes upon governmental action but that have never before been held binding upon nongovernmental institutions. Perhaps the consequence should not frighten us — it is hard to quarrel with the appealing slogan that every enterprise should respect constitutional rights — but I wonder whether we should not pay a heavy price in terms of the loss to the richness, variety, and initiative of our present pluralistic society.

To take a single example, consider the effect upon educational institutions. Though few will defend racial discrimination, one can fairly ask whether Notre Dame should be barred from preferring Roman Catholics or Baylor from giving preference to Baptists. Despite some faults, schools founded for the benefit of particular sects, or even particular social classes, have contributed greatly to American education. Should every school or college be required to permit its property to be used for speeches by Communists, Birchites, Jehovah's Witnesses, and atheists, and men of every political or religious persuasion, if it opens its doors to any? Should its admissions practices and perhaps its examinations be subject to judicial scrutiny for due process of law? Millions of dollars and multitudes of lives have been devoted to pursuing more specialized ideals and benefiting narrower classes than are suitable for governmental activity. They have added immeasurably to the richness of American life.

Similar questions would have to be asked with reference to countless other nongovernmental institutions and activities which would be brought under the constitutional restraints now applied only to governmental action, if the familiar rule were changed. We have hedged government about pretty strictly because of its enormous power and in order to make it the organ of all the people. Today many private organizations have scarcely less power than government to restrict liberty or otherwise affect human rights, but it is far from clear that the constitutional restraints which the Fourteenth Amendment puts upon government are suited to private institutions.

I am not saying that none of the restrictions the constitution puts upon government should ever be applied to private institutions, or that no lines can be drawn between appropriate and inappropriate cases. I do suggest that the judicial process is ill-suited to drawing the lines and that the points of reference supplied by constitutional law are hardly adequate. A legislature may appropriately prohibit discrimination in hotels and motels but tolerate it in rooming houses with six or fewer boarders. A statute may forbid discrimination at theaters but not dance halls, and at lunch counters but not bowling alleys. A legislature may enact an equal-public-accommodations law but reject an open housing measure; it may compromise about discrimination in employment. Of course, the individuals who are judges are usually as well qualified personally to draw such lines as the men who happen to be legislators, but it makes a great difference whether the task is performed in one forum or the other. For a court to draw lines on a legislative basis is unacceptable, partly because the exact location of the line is arbitrary and partly because the preferences upon which even a reasoned determination rests can neither be determined by extrinsic points of reference nor expressed in a standard susceptible of more or less objective application. The task seems even less judicial when one moves away from racial discrimination to other constitutional guarantees.

Once again a word of caution is in order. I do not mean to imply that a rational and coherent body of self-limiting principles cannot possibly be developed that would give effect to the impulses toward loosening the concept of State action under the Fourteenth Amendment. To devise them is one of the current challenges of constitutional litigation. What can be said is that no rationale was offered in the sit-in cases which was not entirely open-ended.

Finally, the sit-in demonstrators faced a series of even harder questions. Granting that the practice of segregation in places of public accommodation was evil, how much of the burden of innovation could the Supreme Court successfully carry? Could a decision sustaining the claim that the Fourteenth Amendment itself required the desegregation of lunch counters and restaurants, without the need for legislative action, have ever commanded the degree of voluntary acceptance necessary to make the prohibition effective law? The response to the school desegregation decisions suggested a negative answer. Would it not be better to leave the question to Congress, which was beginning to bestir itself? In retrospect, it seems clear that the public-accommodations sections of the Civil Rights Act of 1964, after the Supreme Court decision upholding their constitutionality, commanded far wider and deeper acceptance in all parts of the country, because of the participation of all three branches of government, than would have been accorded a Supreme Court ruling sustaining the claim that private establishments were required to desegregate by reason of the Fourteenth Amendment.

It may be argued that with matters in this posture the Court should have had no difficulty in affirming the convictions of the demonstrators. The judiciary, it is often said, should concern itself with law and leave policy to the legislatures. Such a course has much to commend it, but surely rigid adherence to this formula implies too narrow a view of both the function of law and the role of the Court. Constitutional law must grow and change in response to the needs of the community. The Court's influence goes far beyond its writ. Had the Court denied the constitutional claims of the sit-in demonstrators, a lawyer might accurately have said that the decision had nothing to do with morality or policy but represented only the limited function of a constitutional court. In the eyes of laymen and legislators, however, that ruling would have legitimatized the convictions and even the racial discrimination that lay behind them. The force of legality would have influenced both the national consciousness and the debate upon legislative solutions, and would thus have been put to the service of the advocates of segregation. In short, the answer to the question "what substantive rule would be best for the country?" was at odds with that yielded by the inquiry, "policy aside, what decision would be according to law?"

The dilemma is characteristic of constitutional adjudication, yet the tension is seldom so intense. The issue splintered the Court for at least three terms, and the conflict still has repercussions. Although Justices Black and Douglas both condemned the Fabian tactics of the central bloc, they themselves were in disagreement upon the merits. The one clear point, in my view, was that a clear-cut decision either way was wrong and should be avoided if possible — at least so long as there was hope that Congress would outlaw racial discrimination and segregation in places of public accommodation. The ability of the judicial branch to withstand the strains of adjudicating society's most fundamental and divisive public issues is not unlimited. In order to strike effective blows upon critical occasions the Court must be willing, for the most part, to conform its decision to the binding force of law.

Happily, fate brought on for decision, prior to the Civil Rights Act of 1964, only cases which could be decided upon narrow grounds without too much violence to legal doctrine or creating embarrassing precedents. Some went off upon the ground that there was no evidence to sustain conviction for the particular crime charged;[12] others upon the ground that the State statute was unconstitutionally vague or overbroad;[13] still others upon the ground that the State had required or encouraged the operators of restaurants to observe a pattern of segregation.[14] The passage of the Civil Rights Act of 1964 mooted the issue as applied to the sit-in cases because the new statute was held to abate all pending prosecutions.[15]

V

Although the Civil Rights Act of 1964 solved the problem at places of public accommodations, the pressure to extend the promise of *Brown* v. *Board of Education* to other private activities through judicial expansion of the concept of State action remained unabated. None of the decided cases raised problems as broad as those I have been discussing, but two are worthy of consideration.

Evans v. *Newton*[16] concerned land devised to the City of Macon, Georgia, in trust as a "park and pleasure ground" for white people. When it became apparent that the city could not constitutionally administer the park with racial restrictions, the Georgia courts entered a decree accepting the resignation of the city and appointing three private individuals as trustees; presumably they would continue to administer the trust in accordance with the donor's instructions. The Supreme Court of the United States reversed the decree in a 6-3 decision.

The majority opinion by Justice Douglas stands upon two legs.

First, noting that the park was "swept, manicured, watered, patrolled and maintained by the city as a public facility ... as well as granted tax exemption," he ruled that "The momentum it acquired as a public facility is certainly not dissipated ipso facto by the appointment of 'private' trustees. So far as this record shows, there has been no change in municipal maintenance and concern over this facility." If this passage means only that the technical transfer of title is constitutionally irrelevant so long as the premises are treated just like any other municipal park, the case scarcely deserves attention; but the momentum of the past may well turn out to be the decisive element and any change in maintenance and concern may be constitutionally unimportant. Perhaps we shall learn the answer when the *Girard College* case comes back before the Court, for there the question is whether the conduct of a school which was operated by the City of Philadelphia for a century and a half lost the character of State action when private trustees replaced the city.

The other leg of *Evans* v. *Newton* has wider implications. "The service rendered by even a private park of this character is municipal in nature," the Justice said, and "state courts that aid private parties to perform that public function on a segregated basis implicate the State in conduct proscribed by the Fourteenth Amendment." Perhaps a park, like a fire department or police department, is so seldom operated by a private institution that one can fairly characterize it as exclusively governmental, although research might well show that a large number of museums, gardens, historical mansions and like memorials are endowed and managed as private institutions. One suspects, too, that even though Justice Douglas' reasoning was phrased narrowly in this instance, he would regard the point as unimportant. The opinion is strongly reminiscent of the Justice's earlier argument that operating a lunch counter is a government function. It looks ahead to his later opinion in *Reitman* v. *Mulkey* where he argued that the real estate brokers and owners of private housing who practice racial discrimination are engaged in zoning, which is a municipal function, and are therefore subject to the command of the Fourteenth Amendment.

The opinion of the Court in *Reitman* v. *Mulkey*[17] took a much narrower ground. California had been a leader in fair housing legislation and had prohibited racial discrimination in the sale or rental of housing in any dwelling that contained more than four units. The victim of discrimination was given a cause of action against the party practicing it. In November 1964 the people of California, by popular referendum on Proposition 14, amended the State constitution to provide that "neither the State nor any subdivision or agency thereof shall . . . limit . . . the right of any person, who desires to sell, lease or rent any . . . real property, to decline to sell, lease or rent . . . to such person . . . as he, in his absolute discretion chooses."

Subsequently, Negroes who were refused unlet apartments solely upon grounds of color brought an action under the prior California statutes, arguing that the statutory remedies were not eliminated by Proposition 14 because its adoption violated the Fourteenth Amendment to the federal Constitution. The Supreme Court of California sustained their contention. The Supreme Court of the United States, by a 5-4 vote, agreed.

Proposition 14 was a dragon. We shall have neither a great society nor even a modicum of racial calm so long as discrimination in housing breeds urban ghettos. The repeal of open housing laws seems even more dangerous than the failure to enact them. But whether the Supreme Court should play St. George (and, if so, with what weapons it should slay the beast) is quite another question. It is not easy to see how California could fairly be said to deny the Negro plaintiffs "equal protection of the law" merely by refusing to give them aid against the racially motivated refusal to rent an open apartment, when no one who was refused a lease for a nonracial reason would have a cause of action.

The explanation offered in Justice White's opinion for the Court was that no persuasive considerations had been advanced for overturning the belief of the Supreme Court of California that Proposition 14 would "significantly encourage and involve the State in private discriminations." Sufficient involvement to bring the Fourteenth Amendment into play apparently follows from significant encouragement, and what is significant encouragement is treated as at least partly a question of fact. It is hard to believe that even Justice White took this part of his opinion very seriously. Certainly, the concurring justices — Warren, Douglas, Brennan, and Fortas — would not have paused for a moment in reversing a contrary finding by the California court if they had disagreed with it. Nor can anyone suppose that another State, given the same legal situation, would be allowed to conclude that there was no significant encouragement of racial discrimination.

Later in the opinion, in a passage distinguishing the effect of amending the State constitution from the mere repeal of open housing legislation, Justice White vouchsafed his view of the encouragement given by Proposition 14: "Private discriminations in housing were now not only free from Rumford and Unruh but they also enjoyed a far different status than was true before the passage of those statutes. The right to discriminate, including the right to discriminate upon racial grounds, was now embodied *in the State's basic charter* . . . Those practicing racial discriminations *need no longer rely solely on their personal choice.* They could now invoke *express constitutional authority, free from censure or interference of any kind from official sources.*" (Emphasis supplied.)

If these words mean anything, it is that the adoption of Proposition 14 not only withdrew legal constraints but also gave moral support to those who might be tempted to engage in racial discrimination; and apparently it was the second element—the moral support—that Justice White deemed decisive.

The Justice's reasoning leaves me dissatisfied. Is there really any firm basis for concluding that the adoption of Proposition 14 gave more encouragement to acts of private discrimination than would the mere repeal of an open housing law after similar public controversy? What about the defeat of proposed laws against discrimination? In Massachusetts, under certain circumstances, a bill enacted by the legislature and approved by the governor may be rejected at the next election by popular referendum. Suppose the legislature enacted such an open housing law but it was defeated in a referendum. Would not that equally encourage private acts of discrimination? Might not the Massachusetts landlord salve his conscience just as easily as his California counterpart by pointing to the vote of the people? Much the same consequences would attend the defeat of an open housing bill in the legislature itself, after active lobbying and hot and widely publicized debate. The truth would seem to be that the absence of legal restraints gives encouragement of a sort to anyone minded to engage in discrimination, and any defeat of proposed restraints after strong public debate will give moral support to some persons who might not otherwise have been ready to discriminate. The degree of support that is given seems likely to depend upon a congeries of factors far more diffuse and subtle than the differences between repeal of a statute and amendment of a constitution.

One wonders too whether the Court gave enough thought to the implications of placing so much reliance upon the psychological consequences of State action that is otherwise constitutionally unassailable. Is Alabama sufficiently involved in every act of private discrimination within the State to implicate the Fourteenth Amendment because her governor is an outspoken exponent of segregation? Louisiana has a statute declaring segregation of the races to be the official policy of the State. Given this encouragement, does every private person in Louisiana who engages in racial discrimination violate the Fourteenth Amendment? The federal government made much this argument in the sit-in cases, contending that State enactment of the "Jim Crow laws" did so much to establish the caste system reflected by segregation at eating places that the State should not later be permitted to disclaim responsibility with one hand and prosecute the demonstrators with the other. Oddly enough, Justice White joined Justices Black and Harlan in rejecting that contention.

I do not mean to imply that these objections are insuperable. My criticism is that the difficulties were not faced; that the opinion fails to probe the true issues behind the doctrine of State action; that the opinion is inscrutable except as it hints at the proposition that the supposed psychological consequences of a particular bit of State action may render it a violation of the Fourteenth Amendment. The absence of a better rationale invites the cynical charge that the Warren Court is out to slay the dragons without regard to law.

There are times when just such a *coup de main* is required, but *Reitman* v. *Mulkey* hardly presented the occasion. The California situation was unique, and that State can readily repeal the open housing acts. Moreover, there was available a much simpler, narrower, and, at the same time, more direct ground of decision.

Its major premise is that a State violates the equal protection clause if it invidiously discriminates against any race or class of citizens by disabling its legislature, municipal subdivisions, or other organs for the expression of public policy from exercising the same kind of legislative powers in the protection of that particular group as they may generally exercise in behalf of other classes. No precedents lay down this principle, but surely it would violate the Fourteenth Amendment for a southern State to amend its constitution, in a paroxysm of white supremacy, so as to provide that no State law requiring equality of treatment for Negroes in employment, housing, or public accommodations should take effect unless voted by three successive legislatures and signed by three different governors. The constitutional vice would not be psychological encouragement to private discrimination but actual, hostile discrimination against Negroes in the allocation of governmental power.

The minor premise is that Proposition 14 did in fact work such discrimination by disabling the California legislature and municipal bodies from enacting fair housing laws. On its face, Proposition 14 contains no discrimination against any race or other minority. In truth, however, its only effect was to invalidate the Unruh and Rumford open housing laws and to bar all State organs from exercising their normal powers in behalf of the minority groups who might seek the same kind of protective legislation in relation to their need for housing that legislative bodies regularly enact for the benefit of manifold interests in relation to other subjects of legislation. Proposition 14, despite its abstract phrases, was concerned only with racial, and possibly religious, discrimination. Its legal effect was only to disable official organs of the State from exercising their normal powers in a normal fashion for the benefit of such minorities. To take note of this is not to engage in the impermissible process of probing the motives of those who enact legislation or adopt a

constitutional amendment. It is to examine the palpable operative function of the amendment.

The ultimate decision would be the same under either line of
reasoning, but it is not enough for the Court to reach the right
result regardless of how it integrates the decision into the
general body of law. For one thing, candor in facing intellectual
difficulties and professional skill in resolving them are among the
strongest supports of that impartial integrity which distinguishes
judges from legislative representatives and executive officials,
even though such integrity may exist without them.

The craftsmanship—or lack of it—in judicial opinions
strongly influences the judgment that lawyers pass upon the
work of the Court. Professor Richard Neustadt, in writing about
the powers of the President, propounded the thesis that one of
the determinants of what a President can accomplish is the
judgment of a small number of "professionals" upon the professional competence of his performance. The thesis has even
greater validity as applied to the Court, for a large segment of
public opinion looks to lawyers to appraise its performance.

The Court's power to give its decisions the force of legitimacy
ultimately depends in large measure upon its professional artis-
try in weaving wise statecraft into the fabric of law. I cannot
prove the point. Perhaps I, like others who have sensed the
sheer delight of legal reasoning, mistake its importance. But if,
as I suppose, the law is chiefly important as a substitute for and
limitation upon power—and if the capacity of judge-made law to
command free assent depends upon the proposition that the
decisions of judges rest upon principles more enduring and more
general than the wills of individual judges—then the effectiveness of the Court, its very ability to slay the dragons, is eroded
by any failure to show how the novel decisions required by
changes in human condition and the realization of bolder aspira-

tions nonetheless draw their sanction from a continuing community of principle. The more rapid the pace of social change the faster the law must develop. But the faster pace of legal development would seem to create still greater need for striving to preserve, through the articulation of sound rationale, that sense of impartiality and continuity that gives legitimacy, and thus provides the sanction, for the judgments of a court.

No one who has followed the Court's work closely will lightly criticize the reasoning of its opinions. The justices carry the burden of resolving, day after day and week after week, a long succession of issues, each one of which occupies the professor-critic for months and even years of specialized study. I am aware too that the shortcomings of judicial opinions often reflect the inadequacies of counsel, for I have had to recall that my own briefs as an advocate failed to deal with some of the difficulties with opinions that bother me as a professor. Opinions of the Court, moreover, must be written to win the assent of at least five justices even when there is no genuine consensus about the reasons to be given or perhaps even about the decision to rendered. We tend to forget the difficulty of massing a majority within the Court and the wisdom, even the necessity, of postponing or evading fundamental issues.

Several of these forces must have been operative in *Reitman* v. *Mulkey*. Justice White was apparently necessary to make up the five-man majority; yet his votes in the sit-in cases indicate that he would have been unwilling to join in putting the decision upon any of the broader grounds that might have been embraced by the other four.

Finally, one may surmise that the want of an adequate rationale for the decision in *Reitman* v. *Mulkey* may also be attributable to the need to work out principles defining the operative scope of two basic ideas underlying much of the work of the

Warren Court. One is the spirit of egalitarianism. The other is a growing but unarticulated sense that some of the affirmative obligations of modern government may, in the case of the States, be appropriately incorporated into the constitutional duties imposed by the Fourteenth Amendment. We can hardly expect a logical pattern of decisions upon the extent of State responsibility for private action until the operative limitations of those ideas have emerged not merely in substantive terms but in respect to the relative functions of the legislative and judicial branches.

3 Civil Rights: Legislative Power

ALTHOUGH THE SCHOOL DESEGREGATION CASES condemned racial discrimination in any activities of government, the decision had no direct effect upon the broader reaches of our social and economic system where activities of enormous public consequence are conducted by individuals and private (*i.e.* nongovernmental) institutions. The power of the States to strike at such pillars of the caste system as segregation and discrimination in places of public accommodation, in employment, and in housing cannot be seriously questioned, but no one has ever seriously supposed that all the States would exercise the power. The elimination of these injustices can be accomplished within the frame of law only through the intervention of a national government.

Thus far the pressure has fallen upon both the judicial and legislative branches. The Supreme Court could conceivably take the leadership by abolishing the requirement of "State action" and applying the equal protection clause directly to many forms of essentially private discrimination without legislative action. The obstacles inherent in the nature of the judicial process were discussed in the previous lecture. Legislative action would be a much sounder method of imposing new and pervasive restrictions upon the conduct of business enterprises, if one could judge soundness exclusively in terms of the distribution of functions among the three branches of government. But efforts to provide a national legislative remedy encountered constitutional obstacles in terms of the established distribution of power between the Nation and the States. Thus the need for Congress to provide national solutions to the problems of race relations is exerting great influence upon the balance of power in the federal system.

I

The only major federal legislation dealing with private racial discrimination—the Civil Rights Act of 1964—rests primarily upon Article I, Section 8, of the Constitution, which gives Congress power "to regulate commerce . . . among the several states." Title II of the Act prohibits racial segregation or discrimination in places of public accommodation. The prohibition was attacked as unconstitutional by Ollie McClung in Birmingham.[1] Much of the meat served in Ollie's Barbecue came from outside Alabama, but, so far as he knew, Ollie had no out-of-state customers. The decision sustaining the application of the federal statute to Ollie's choice of customers as a regulation of interstate commerce strikes many nonlawyers as a complete distortion of the words "to regulate commerce . . . among the several states," just as it shocks law students until their professors corrupt them. Actually the decision did little more than dramatize four settled principles of constitutional law established late in the 1930's:

(1) Congress may regulate any activity, however local, that affects interstate commerce.[2]

(2) The judicial branch will not review a congressional determination that a local activity affects interstate commerce if

there are any data affording rational support for that determination.[3]

(3) Questions of proximity and degree are also exclusively for the legislature. The Court will not invalidate an act of Congress merely because the activity is predominantly local and its effect upon commerce is remote.[4]

(4) Congressional regulation of a local practice potentially affecting the interstate movement of goods will be upheld without investigating whether the predominant purpose and effect of the measure are local and noncommercial.[5] It was therefore constitutionally irrelevant, even if it were true, that the aim of the equal-public-accommodations law was to eliminate racial segregation from local places of public accommodation upon any available excuse.

For the Court to reemphasize those propositions just before it began to elaborate the power of Congress under Section 5 of the Fourteenth Amendment turned out to be highly useful. The scope of the latter power is likely to depend upon the extent to which the same propositions are applied *mutis mutandis*. Except for this, I would be inclined to regret the decision to defend the constitutionality of the equal-public-accommodations law primarily by analogy to the National Labor Relations Act, upon the ground that segregation in restaurants threatens to curtail their purchases of food moving in interstate commerce not only by limiting their patronage but also by creating the threat of disruptive demonstrations. The parallel was close; restaurants indistinguishable from Ollie's Barbecue had been held subject to NLRB jurisdiction[6] and a demonstration protesting racial discrimination among potential customers would have about the same effect upon interstate commerce as picketing to protest discrimination against union members among the employees. Concern for the interstate flow of goods, though a jurisdictional prerequisite, is hardly the real reason for extending NLRB jurisdiction to local retail establishments; that, too, has a local purpose — protecting union organization because the protection is fair to employees and secures their welfare regardless of the effect upon interstate commerce. But the use of a basis for jurisdiction that had come to be accepted without question in the labor cases is often regarded as disingenuous in the racial context. It might therefore have been better to have defended the statute upon the more forthright but less familiar ground that Congress has ample power to secure all persons equal access as consumers to the fruits of interstate commerce even in the ultimate stages of distribution, just as it has the admitted authority to secure equality in travel accommodations.[7]

Other legislation aimed at securing equality of opportunity in the private sector — for example, a federal open housing law — could probably be sustained under the commerce clause; but the effort, as with the equal-public-accommodations law, would seem to stretch the clause to the point of distortion. The Fourteenth Amendment, if available, is a more natural source of power, for its policy, within its scope, is equality among the races. It may be the only source of national authority to protect Negroes and civil rights workers against violence or economic reprisals.

II

In this respect, the words of the Fourteenth Amendment — and until recently the precedents — were rather discouraging. Section 1 is addressed to the States — not to private individuals.

> No State shall ... deny to any person ... equal protection of the laws.

Section 5 gives Congress only the power

> to enforce, by appropriate legislation, the provisions of this article.

Moreover, the precedents epitomized by the *Civil Rights Cases*[8] established the doctrine that Congress has no power to legislate under Section 5 unless a State is in violation of Section 1.[9] So long as the precedents stood, Congress could do little, apart from the commerce clause, to legislate against racial reprisals or private discrimination.

Two uncontrovertible facts argue against the doctrine of the *Civil Rights Cases* as a restraint upon congressional power: (1) racial justice is in fact a national problem; (2) without federal legislative action the civil rights revolution cannot be accomplished within a framework of law. Under the pressure of these facts, which are stronger than any theory, the older doctrine is eroding and the Warren Court is reshaping constitutional law so as to provide a Fourteenth Amendment basis for federal legislation securing racial equality in the private sector. The same decisions, as I read them, also begin to lay the constitutional foundation for federal legislation securing other fundamental human rights.

III

The first case seems a little remote because it deals with voting rights—and with the Fifteenth Amendment, not the Fourteenth—but it is important nonetheless because it gives broad scope to a grant of power "to enforce, by appropriate legislation." By 1965 suits brought in Alabama, Mississippi, and

Louisiana to enjoin practices depriving Negroes of the right to vote on the ground of race or color proved that the chief engines of discrimination were literacy tests and like devices, such as requiring the voter to demonstrate his ability to interpret and understand the State constitution. Fair on their face, these laws vested uncontrolled discretion in the county registrars in selecting the provisions to be interpreted, in giving or withholding assistance, and in grading the answers. The registrars put them to their intended use. The Voting Rights Act of 1965 automatically suspended the use of all such tests and devices, including all literacy tests, in any State or county as to which the Attorney General determined that a test or device had been in force and the Director of the Census certified that less than fifty percent of the adult population had voted in the presidential election of 1964. The theory was that these findings marked the areas in which there was reason to believe that the tests might be used for racial discrimination.

In an original suit in the Supreme Court, South Carolina challenged the power of Congress to suspend the use of a State literacy test for voting in State elections, where the test was fair on its face and there had been no judicial finding of racial discrimination. The issue turned upon the meaning of Section 2 of the Fifteenth Amendment. Section 1 forbids the States to deny United States citizens the right to vote on account of race or color, and Section 2 adds:

> The Congress shall have power to enforce this article by appropriate legislation.

South Carolina's chief argument was in two steps: (1) the "power to enforce" is confined to punishing or redressing actual discrimination in voting and cannot be used as a source of authority to enact prophylactic measures; (2) South Carolina had not been proved ever to have used her literacy test as an engine of racial discrimination.

The United States, relying chiefly upon the analogy to the commerce and "necessary and proper" clauses, replied that Congress is not confined to dealing with actual discrimination in voting but may regulate or prohibit any conduct which creates a danger of discrimination: "Congress may employ means which, 'although not themselves within the granted power, were nevertheless deemed appropriate aids to the accomplishment of some purpose within an admitted power of the national government.' "[10]

The Court accepted this broad interpretation. "The basic test to be applied in a case involving §2 of the Fifteenth Amendment," the Chief Justice declared, "is the same as in all cases concerning the express powers of Congress in relation to the reserved powers of the States"; and he then quoted Marshall's classic expression:

> Let the end be legitimate, let it be within the scope of the constitution, and all means which are appropriate, which are plainly adapted to that end, which are not prohibited, but consist with the letter and spirit of the constitution, are constitutional.[11]

The potential scope of *South Carolina* v. *Katzenbach* became apparent in *Katzenbach* v. *Morgan.*[12] At issue was Section 4(e) of the Voting Rights Act, which provided that no person who had successfully completed the sixth grade in a Puerto Rican school where instruction was in Spanish should be denied the right to vote because of inability to read or write English. The provision enfranchised thousands of Spanish-speaking citizens who had moved to New York from Puerto Rico but had been barred from voting by a New York statute requiring literacy in English. The Court upheld the federal statute under Section 5 of the Fourteenth Amendment. The principal branch of the opinion sustains congressional removal of the State's requirement of English literacy on the ground that Congress might have viewed the removal as a measure adapted to securing the Puerto Ricans residing in New York against unconstitutional discrimination in the provision of government services, such as public schools, public housing, and law enforcement. Even if the requirement of literacy did not itself deny equal protection, the Court said, the practical effect of abolishing the requirement was to enfranchise large segments of New York's Puerto Rican community. "This enhanced political power will be helpful in gaining nondiscriminatory treatment in public services for the entire Puerto Rican community. Section 4(e) thereby enables the Puerto Rican minority better to obtain 'perfect equality of civil rights and equal protection of the laws.' "[13]

In my opinion, this ruling provides a secure basis for upholding the constitutionality of federal legislation prohibiting racial discrimination in the sale or rental of housing. If Congress may legislate to remove the requirement of English literacy as a prerequisite to voting in State elections as an obstacle to the State's performance of its constitutional duty not to discriminate in providing public services, even though the immediate subject matter of the legislation—the requirement of English literacy—is not itself a violation of the Fourteenth Amendment, then Congress must have the same power to eliminate racial ghettos, which are also obstacles to the States' performance of the constitutional duty to provide equal public services, even though the immediate subject matter of this legislation—the private racial discrimination that results in ghettos—does not itself violate the amendment.

The only difference is that in *Katzenbach* v. *Morgan* the obstacle was a State law whereas discrimination in housing is the work of private citizens. The difference in the source of the threat to performance of the State's obligation seems irrelevant to the constitutional question, however, so long as the congressional objective is to secure performance of the State's indubitable constitutional obligation not to discriminate in providing public services. Even if State involvement in creating racial discrimination be necessary to make out a violation of the equal protection clause, because its words lay the prohibition only upon State action, still nothing in Section 5 confines Congress to dealing with State action in enacting legislation that provides greater assurance that the State will comply with its constitutional duty. Private persons who join with State officials in violating constitutional rights have been held subject to federal prosecution.[14] Federal judicial power has been exercised against private persons who obstruct State officials in the performance of their constitutional duty.[15] There would seem to be ample power, therefore, to forbid discrimination by owners, operators, or brokers in the sale or rental of housing as means of facilitating the break-up of racial ghettos and thus enabling Negroes "better to obtain 'perfect equality of civil rights and equal protection of the laws.' "[16]

The potentialities that *Katzenbach* v. *Morgan* logically opens for a vast expansion of federal power are by no means confined to race relations. They extend, for example, to a code of criminal procedure applicable to State prosecutions. Under recent decisions the general guarantee of "due process of law" creates many specific federal rights,[17] and there are few aspects of a trial that are not sufficiently connected with one or another of the federal rights for Congress to regulate them as a way of facilitating fuller realization of the constitutional guarantee. For the moment, however, there is no reason to suppose that Congress will choose thus to invade a traditional province of the States.

IV

Whatever doubt the *Morgan* case left concerning the power of Congress to reach private racial discrimination under Section 5 of the Fourteenth Amendment where necessary to prevent unconstitutional State action was laid to rest by the opinions of six justices in *United States* v. *Guest*[18] — the third, and thus far the last, step in extending the power of Congress to deal with private action that interferes with the enjoyment of fundamental human rights. Colonel Penn, a Negro, had been murdered while driving through Georgia on his way to Washington, D.C., after a tour of military duty. Guest and his codefendants, who were charged with the shooting, were tried for murder under Georgia law, but they were also indicted by the United States for violating Section 241 of the Criminal Code by conspiring to oppress or intimidate a citizen in his enjoyment of "rights secured by the Constitution or laws of the United States." The indictment alleged that one object of the conspiracy was to bar the exercise of the "right to the equal utilization, without discrimination upon the basis of race, of public facilities . . . owned, operated or managed by or on behalf of the State of Georgia or any subdivision . . ."[19]

All the defendants were private persons. There was no suggestion that Georgia was not offering equal facilities and doing everything appropriate to protect Negroes in their enjoyment. Had the defendants been the only conspirators, two questions would have been presented:

(1) whether Section 241 applies to private conspiracies to

interfere with the enjoyment of such Fourteenth Amendment rights as equal access to schools, golf courses, and other public facilities; and

(2) whether Congress has power to enact such legislation.

A majority of the justices intimated a negative answer on the first point but, in the end, they avoided any necessity for deciding either question by construing the indictment to allege that unnamed State officials were parties to the conspiracy. Justice Brennan, speaking for the Chief Justice and Justice Douglas and himself, gave an affirmative answer to the first question and concluded that the statute, thus construed, was constitutional. This impelled Justice Clark, joined by Justices Black and Fortas, to declare *obiter dictum* that they too were convinced that "the specific language of §5 empowers the Congress to enact laws punishing all conspiracies — with or without state action — that interfere with Fourteenth Amendment rights."[20]

It is hard to know what the six justices — three from the majority and three in dissent — meant by this declaration. Novel and important as the ruling might be, none of them thought it deserved a full exposition. Possibly they meant only that Congress has power to punish those who resort to violence or other forms of intimidation to prevent the desegregation of schools and other government facilities. Thus limited, the dictum would overturn a number of precedents,[21] but the overruling would hardly signify a constitutional revolution. Congress may provide for punishing mob action aimed at preventing school authorities from admitting Negroes to once-segregated schools, for this is an appropriate measure for securing the authorities' performance of their Fourteenth Amendment duties.[22] There is scant practical difference between private violence barring the authorities from opening the schools and private violence aimed at preventing Negroes from attending the officially desegregated institutions. Earlier the creation of other rights against the government — such as the right to take up a homestead upon public lands — had been held to put duties upon private persons to refrain from aggression.[23] Only those who view constitutional law as exclusively an exercise in logic could deny the impelling need, at a time when we are seeking to accomplish a civil rights revolution within the frame of law, for federal power to secure the safety of those who exercise their constitutional rights — not as a substitute for local law enforcement but as visible proof that if local officials are inadequate, slothful, or conniving, still an impartial rule of law may be preserved. The immediate accretion to federal power is microscopic in relation to the vast aggregate already exercised even in the field of criminal law. If nothing more were involved, therefore, it would be easy to agree with Justice Brennan that no principle of federalism denies Congress power to punish individuals who are neither State officers nor acting in concert with State officers when they conspire to threaten, harass, and murder Negroes for attempting to enjoy equal use of State facilities.

V

In my view much more was involved. I expect the fulfillment of events to show that when the six justices said in *Guest* that Congress has power to deal with "all conspiracies — with or without state action — that interfere with Fourteenth Amendment rights" they meant *all* Fourteenth Amendment rights. And once that conclusion is reached, there is no possible reason to distinguish between conspiracies and individual action, or between violence and other forms of interference.

A few examples will illustrate the potentialities. If my analysis is correct, the constitutionality of federal legislation prohibiting discrimination in the sale and rental of housing can readily be sustained under Section 5 of the Fourteenth Amendment as a means of protecting the civil right of Negroes to own, buy, and sell all kinds of real and personal property, everywhere, equally with whites. One of the major purposes of the amendment was to secure Negroes this legal right in State law. A conspiracy to deter Negroes, by violence or threats of violence, from buying property anywhere in a community would be a proper subject of federal cognizance because the conspiracy would defeat the practical enjoyment of the legal right, even though the right survived conceptually. That is *Guest,* save that the hypothetical conspiracy is aimed at depriving Negroes of enjoyment of the Fourteenth Amendment right to own property rather than to use public facilities. Surely the case is the same if the whole community substitutes for violence an express conspiracy or unspoken custom of refusing to sell any property to any Negroes; the scope of the power of Congress does not depend upon whether it is forbidding aggressive acts or imposing affirmative duties. One's impression is quite different if he thinks of a single refusal to sell and unconsciously assumes that ample property of every description is otherwise available, for in that event to speak of diminution of the civil right to buy and sell seems artificial. The actual state of affairs doubtless varies from one community to another and often lies between the two extremes. But if Congress thinks that private discrimination in the sale or rental of housing substantially interferes with the Negroes' enjoyment of an equal right to buy and sell property, the judiciary can hardly disagree; finding the facts and appraising their significance is a legislative function. Furthermore, Congress may regulate individual instances which lack significance when taken in isolation, if cumulatively their regulation is appropriate to effectuating a constitutional objective.[24]

One wonders, if the reasoning behind the *Guest* pronouncement extends this far, whether it is limited to the equal protection clause or also enables Congress to legislate against private interference with the enjoyment of rights protected by the due process clause. Conceivably, the courts might draw a distinction upon Justice Bradley's initial theory that the equal protection clause, like the Fifteenth Amendment, uses a double negative—the State shall not deny—which implies an affirmative duty,[25] whereas the due process clause imposes only negative restrictions. Justice Bradley later rejected his own reasoning, however, and it seems more likely today that whatever protection against private persons Congress can give the victims of invidious discrimination it can also extend to those whom private persons deprive of the enjoyment of the rights of life, liberty, and property. On this theory federal legislation could be enacted which punished private persons who sought to silence an unpopular speaker or to suppress the exercise of religion. Logically, it would seem that larceny and other crimes against property could thus be brought within the federal domain.

For Congress to enact and the Court to uphold such legislation upon a wide scale would revolutionize our federal system. For the Court to hold that Congress has such authority, even though it is seldom exercised, implies a revolutionary change in the distribution of governmental power. The State-action concept was advanced in debates over the proposed Fourteenth Amendment and later accepted by the Supreme Court in the *Civil Rights Cases* because of the fear that any relaxation of the requirement of State action would logically lead to the conclusion that Congress might "establish a code of municipal law regulative of all private rights between man and man" and thus "take the place of State legislatures."[26] Perhaps it is "far out" to conclude that the *Guest* case now supports just that implication, but a number of considerations suggest that the power is there if Congress chooses to exercise it sparingly.

In the first place the pronouncement in *Guest* crosses a watershed in logical analysis. To speak simply of "Fourteenth Amendment rights" is ambiguous. There are at least two kinds of rights: rights good against all the world and rights *in personam* good against particular persons or organizations. To define the character of a particular right one must look to the correlative duty. The Fourteenth Amendment says nothing of rights; it speaks only of duties and it lays duties only upon the State. The exactly correlative rights are to have the State perform its duties. In the *Guest* case Georgia was performing its duty: she had opened her public facilities to Negroes upon equal terms with whites and, so far as appears, she offered Negroes the same protection in the enjoyment of the facilities as any other citizen. The six justices leapt over the logical gap created by the absence of any breach of constitutional duty by speaking objectively of "Fourteenth Amendment rights" as if they were rights against all the world. Perhaps a more logical bridge could be constructed. Once one has got over the gap in one case, however, by saying that the power to enforce the State's duty includes authority to prevent private interference with the enjoyment of the facilities the State offers, there is no longer any logical or conceptual obstacle to Congress's removing private obstructions to the enjoyment of any other constitutional guarantee.

Of course, constitutional law need not press logic to its limits. Justice Holmes once countered a too logical application of Chief Justice Marshall's dictum that the power to tax involves the power to destroy by observing—"not...while this Court sits."[27] But the pragmatic distinctions that might be used to limit

Guest are not in keeping with constitutional trends, even though they may be eminently sensible in framing legislation.

In the *Guest* case the allegations of conspiracy implied a conscious purpose to interfere with the exercise of constitutional rights, but if Congress may deal with private interference, without State action, the difference between intentional, negligent or accidental interference can hardly have constitutional significance.

In the *Guest* case there was a somewhat special relationship between the State and the citizens who were seeking to enjoy the facilities it offered, just as there is between the State and a prisoner in custody, but not between the State and every individual within the jurisdiction. An alternative formula suggests that in *Guest* the "real" federal concern was indeed the desegregation of State facilities whereas the "real" aim of open housing legislation would not be so much to secure recognition of the legal power to buy and sell property as to eliminate the consequences of private discrimination, just as the "real" purpose of a federal law punishing horse-stealing could hardly be to secure the owner in his constitutional right not to have his horse taken by the State without just compensation. Both formulas, so far as I can see, are really ways of expressing judgments of proximity and degree. In the famous *Schechter Poultry* case[28] and again in the original *Labor Board Cases*[29] the Court asserted judicial power to draw such judgments under the commerce clause, but it soon became apparent that the necessary lines could not be drawn by the judiciary, and passing upon such questions of degree and relative importance became a legislative function. The opinion in *Katzenbach* v. *Morgan* makes it plain that the Court presently expects to follow the same course in reviewing legislation enacted under Section 5 of the Fourteenth Amendment.

A number of long-range, fundamental forces also suggest the likelihood of further evolution of constitutional doctrines sustaining congressional power to remove private barriers to racial equality and to the exercise of other fundamental human rights, provided only that the legislation is linked to the practical enjoyment of some obligation that the Fourteenth Amendment lays upon the States. Race relations are a national problem. Further congressional action will be required to bring the civil rights revolution to a just conclusion within the rule of law. But the sense that government has an obligation to make affirmative provision for the enjoyment of human rights goes beyond racial equality. We have become accustomed to the idea that government is responsible for the level of economic activity and should provide education, welfare, medical assistance, housing, and jobs. We also recognize that, although the chief threat to individual freedom in the realm of the spirit once seemed to come only from government, today such liberties are sometimes threatened by the power of labor unions, business corporations, and other organizations. It seems inevitable, in this milieu, that the idea should develop that government has both the right and obligation to secure freedom and equality beyond the realm of governmental action. And, since those human liberties have long enjoyed constitutional status, it is natural that the government's obligation to protect them should develop as part of constitutional law.

This kind of development is better suited to legislative than judicial action. Constitutional government must operate by consent of the governed. Judge-made law draws no authority from the participation of the people. A legislative enactment establishing new standards for the promotion of human rights will command more acceptance, once stamped with the judicial imprimatur of constitutionality, than novel doctrine enunciated by the Court. The impulses leading to the expansion of such constitutional rights appear not to contain their own limitations. The lines that must be drawn lend themselves better to the arbitrariness of political adjustment than to the rationalization of a systematic body of judge-made law. Congress has far greater flexibility in framing remedies and providing for their administration, especially remedies correcting the underlying social and economic conditions. Since Congress is charged with legislative responsibility for the constitutional rights secured by the Fourteenth Amendment, these are strong reasons for encouraging legislative initiative. If Congress would provide the necessary remedies, it would relieve the pressure upon the Court. Thus the strain of the sit-in cases undoubtedly explains the expansion of congressional power in *Morgan* and *Guest*.

Of course, any such development would give new power to the national government, but that trend too is in keeping with other, more powerful forces. The need for vast public expenditures, coupled with the relative ease with which the federal government can raise money, involves Washington in thousands of once-local functions. The improvement of transportation and communication puts Washington in quicker and closer touch with every corner of the country in 1967 than State capitals were with cities within the same State a century earlier. The emergence of national markets, coupled with increasing appreciation of economic interdependence, led to the enormous expansion of federal power under the commerce clause. The Court has already vastly extended national judicial supervision over the States under the due process and equal protection clauses. There is no reason to suppose that further legislative development would be much different under Section 5 of the Fourteenth Amendment.

Nor should we be misled by the extent of the power which my

interpretation of *Guest* vests in Congress. The possession of congressional power is not to be confused with its exercise. Logically, Congress can regulate every detail of almost every commercial transaction, and as an incident of that regulation it can probably deal with the acquisition and ownership of property. It has not exercised its full power, at least partly because of concern for the balance of the federal system. The Court's responsibility for the long-range structure of government requires it to consider the distribution of power not only between Nation and State but also between the legislative and judicial branches. Whatever balance the Court might prefer to see struck between State and Nation, it must also remember that choosing the means of achieving permissible objectives is a legislative function. To that extent preserving constitutional allocation of power between Court and Congress requires allocating to Congress much of the responsibility for the federal system. Congress may ignore the values of federalism and abuse its power, but against that danger, as John Marshall told us, the restraints are solely the "wisdom and the discretion of Congress, their identity with the people, and the influence which their constituents possess at elections . . . They are the restraints on which the people must often rely solely, in all representative governments."[30]

VI

It is ironic that the decisions in *South Carolina* v. *Katzenbach, Katzenbach* v. *Morgan,* and *United States* v. *Guest,* which go so far to secure Congress adequate legislative power to promote racial equality in the private sectors of society, should have been decided in the very year in which began the sharp political reaction against the civil rights movement. The law must ultimately fulfill the promise of *Brown* v. *Board of Education* in both the governmental and private sectors of society. Legislative redress is more flexible and more effective than judicial intervention. The contrast between the Court's restraint in the sit-in cases and its expansive pronouncements concerning congressional power under Section 5 of the Fourteenth Amendment demonstrates its preference for congressional solutions even in the area of constitutional rights. But neither legislative nor popular inaction will dissipate the moral pressure for racial justice. If Congress will not act, the pressure will fall upon the Court to provide relief directly by interpretations of the Fourteenth Amendment which not only relax or even abolish the requirement of State action as a prerequisite to judicial involvement but also expand the State's constitutional duties to include the correction of inequalities built into the existing system, such as the *de facto* school segregation resulting from residential patterns developed by private prejudice and economic forces.

Perhaps the Court should not and will not act where Congress refuses, but the student of recent constitutional history will observe that the Warren Court has been most activist in areas where politicians were blind to fundamental injustice.

4 The Reform of Criminal Procedure

A DECADE AGO THE SUPREME COURT began the widespread reform of criminal procedure in both the State and federal courts. Federal prosecutions are subject to its general supervisory authority, which extends to all matters of procedure and evidence not governed by specific legislation. State prosecutions, however, lie beyond the supervisory power, for in this area the States are sovereign — subject only to constitutional limitations. The States' administration of criminal law is many, many times more important than any federal jurisdiction, for the States are charged with preserving public order and maintaining the security of persons, property, and normal commercial transactions. If the Supreme Court was to influence these major aspects of the administration of criminal justice in State tribunals, it would have to act through constitutional law.

The vehicle became the Fourteenth Amendment's command that —

> No state shall . . . deprive any person of life, liberty, or property, without due process of law . . .

The amendment had long been used to condemn a few extraordinary excesses in State procedure, but the settled view, as expressed by Justice Cardozo in *Palko* v. *Connecticut*,[1] was that the amendment did not enforce upon the States the relatively specific guarantees of the federal Bill of Rights, such as the necessity for indictment by a grand jury, trial by petit jury, and the prohibition against double jeopardy. Rather the amendment protected rights on the "different plane of social and moral values" which might be described as "the very essence of a scheme of ordered liberty" and "so rooted in the traditions and conscience of our people as to be ranked as fundamental." The formula proved flexible enough for progressively tightening the constitutional rules applicable to State procedure and this has been one vehicle of reform, but it implied a theory of federalism that restricted the Supreme Court's role in favor of vesting responsibility and discretion in the States.

The thrust of the doctrinal changes, therefore, centered upon repudiation of the *Palko* doctrine. In 1947 Justice Black's famous dissent in *Adamson* v. *California*[2] argued that *Palko* was wrong and that the Fourteenth Amendment did indeed take up and apply to the States each of the relatively specific guarantees of the federal Bill of Rights. He based his argument partly on a reading of history and partly on the thesis that the judges could find closer guidance in the words of the Constitution than in roaming through individual notions of ordered liberty. Justice Black's view has never commanded an open majority of the justices, but enough of them to hold the balance of power have gone part way by espousing a doctrine of selective incorporation under which individual provisions of the Bill of Rights are held to be incorporated into the Fourteenth Amendment.[3] The cynically minded might suggest that the doctrine of selective incorporation is only a Khrushchevian device for effectuating the Black position a slice at a time: thus far its exponents have not found a provision that should not be selectively incorporated. The theory, taken at face value, lacks even the historical warrant that Justice Black could assemble, and it does little to avoid the vagaries of individual judgment beyond channeling them into the process of selection. Whatever its defects as constitutional theory, however, selective incorporation has been a second important vehicle for the reform of criminal law.

The third vehicle is the expansion of the requirements of the Bill of Rights as applied to both State and federal prosecutions.

II

The catalog of changes wrought by these doctrinal instruments would be too familiar for review if it were not for the impact that is achieved by looking simultaneously at the total body of reforms.

Throughout our constitutional history men too poor to retain counsel had been put on trial in many States without the assistance of an attorney, even men charged with serious, albeit not capital, crimes. The constitutionality of the practice had been sustained in numerous cases.[4] Since *Gideon* v. *Wainwright*[5] — a story celebrated in Anthony Lewis' fascinating book *Gideon's Trumpet* — indigents must be supplied with counsel at public expense in all serious criminal cases. The same rule applies to the provision of transcripts[6] and lawyers for appeal.[7]

No longer may a State Court follow the prevailing and apparently well-settled practice of allowing the police to use evidence obtained by an unlawful arrest or by entering a house without a warrant.[8] The requirements for obtaining arrest warrants and search warrants have been stiffened.[9] In other cases the Court, again overruling a long line of precedents, extended to State prosecutions the same privilege against self-incrimination that prevails in the federal courts, including freedom from comment upon the accused's failure to testify in his own defense.[10] The law of confessions has been rewritten.[11] A start has been made upon developing standards governing the admission and exclusion of evidence obtained by wiretapping and other forms of electronic surveillance.[12] There has been far closer scrutiny of the observance of constitutional standards relating to: conduct of the prosecutor in using, revealing, or withholding evidence;[13] selection of the jury;[14] the privilege of confronting adverse witnesses;[15] and the right to compulsory process in order to obtain witnesses for the defense.[16] Another precedent-breaking decision put proceedings against juveniles under many of the safeguards applicable to ordinary criminal cases.[17]

Never has there been such a thorough-going reform of criminal procedure within so short a time. Nearly all the changes benefit the accused. To discuss them in detail is not feasible. Two deserve attention: the problem of electronic eavesdropping, because of its intrinsic interest, and the law of confessions, because it epitomizes the trend.

III

Constitutional law about wiretapping begins with the era of prohibition. In the *Olmstead* case[18] a five-man majority led by Chief Justice Taft held that the Fourth Amendment's guarantee of the "right of the people to be secure in their persons, houses, papers, and effects, against unreasonable searches and seizures" was not violated by federal officials tapping telephone wires in order to obtain evidence of rum-running, because listening to telephone conversations involved no physical trespass to the premises or property of the defendants. The same principle would permit the police to eavesdrop by "bugs" put upon the outer wall of a room, or by a parabolic microphone which can pick up a conversation hundreds of feet away, or by wiring an informer for sound and sending him to talk with suspected criminals while a hidden recorder takes down the conversation and a tiny transmitter, likewise concealed, broadcasts it to the waiting receivers of government agents. The application of the *Olmstead* principle to these practices was sustained in later cases.[19]

The first limitations upon *Olmstead* were imposed under the Federal Communications Act. Section 605 provides that "no person . . . shall intercept any [wire] communication and divulge or publish the existence, contents, purport, effect or meaning . . ." *Nardone* v. *United States*[20] held that Section 605 applies to federal officials and requires the reversal of any criminal conviction based upon evidence which is the fruit of a violation. There are three important limitations, however, upon the scope of the ruling. First, since it rests upon the Communications Act, it applies only to the interception of wire communications and leaves all other forms of eavesdropping unrestricted. Second, even as applied to wire communications, it was interpreted by Attorney General Robert H. Jackson to forbid only interception *and* divulgence; there is no divulgence and therefore no illegality, he said, in federal agents' tapping telephone conversations and reporting the contents within the executive departments. The opinion of the Attorney General was given under the pressures of wartime fears of espionage and subversion, but it laid the foundation for the recent controversial eavesdropping in investigations of organized crime. Third, the *Nardone* ruling did not necessarily bar the use of wiretap evidence in the State courts.

The result was inconsistency, immorality, and intolerable confusion. Under a dubious interpretation of the Communications Act the federal government engaged in wiretapping of which it was ashamed as dirty business. The interpretation made legality depend upon shrouding the practice in secrecy; yet it is secrecy that creates the greatest fears of abuse if not the actual abuses. State officials practiced wiretapping, often in ways regularized and sanctioned by State law, and they used the evidence in court. Federal prosecutors could hardly prosecute them for thus discovering proof of crime, even though their conduct plainly violated the Communications Act, for it was substantially similar to federal practices authorized by the Attorney General. Meanwhile, individual opinions written by Supreme Court justices criticizing eavesdropping made it doubtful whether *Olmstead* continued to command a majority of the Court.

Bringing order into this confusion will require a combination of federal legislation and constitutional interpretation. Three cases suggest that at least the broad outlines of the constitutional position have begun to emerge.

In the first place, it is probably constitutional to use tape and wire recordings to verify the oral testimony of a witness concerning a conversation in which he openly participated. In *Lopez* v. *United States*[21] a taxpayer under investigation by the Internal Revenue Service invited the agent to his office in a manner suggesting that he would seek to bribe the agent. The agent reported to his superiors and then accepted the invitation equipped with a concealed recorder. At a subsequent trial for attempted bribery, the agent testified and the recording was introduced in evidence over the taxpayer's objection that its use violated his constitutional rights. The jury returned a verdict of guilty. The Supreme Court affirmed the conviction over the dissents of Justices Douglas, Brennan, and Goldberg. The decision seems likely to stand. As the Chief Justice said in a special concurrence, the only purpose the recording serves in such circumstances is to protect the credibility of a witness against that of a man who, if the recording be believed, was seeking to corrupt the witness in the performance of a public trust. Presumably the doctrine goes beyond attempts at bribery. No man should have a constitutional right to the assurance that, if he denies what other participants in a conversation disclose, none shall produce an accurate record of the words.

The second case arose out of the prosecution of James Hoffa in Nashville, Tennessee. An investigator hired by Osborn, Hoffa's attorney, reported to an agent of the Department of Justice that when he told Osborn of his close acquaintance with three prospective jurors, Osborn proposed that he arrange a bribe. The information was presented in a sworn affidavit to two federal judges who then gave instructions to have the investigator carry a concealed recorder at later meetings with Osborn. Subsequently the recordings were used to corroborate the investigator's testimony at Osborn's trial. The evidence was damning. Osborn was convicted. The Supreme Court ultimately held that the recording was properly admitted in evidence.[22] The opinion noted that its use was sanctioned by the *Lopez* case but put the decision upon the narrower ground that the central requirement of the Fourth Amendment — authorization for the search by an independent magistrate upon a showing of justification — was satisfied by the submission of a "detailed factual affidavit alleging the commission of a specific criminal offense" and by the district judges' authorization of use of the recorder "for the narrow and particularized purpose of ascertaining the truth of the affidavit's allegations." Only Justice Douglas dissented.

The third case, *Berger* v. *New York*,[23] makes explicit the inference that could be drawn from the *Osborn* opinion—that the Court had resolved to assimilate secret electronic surveillance of private conversations to the trespassory searches and seizures in terms of which the Framers wrote the Fourth Amendment. A New York statute empowered State judges to enter *ex parte* orders authorizing secret surveillance and recording of conversations upon application of a district attorney or ranking police officer supported by an affidavit that "there is reasonable ground to believe that evidence of crime may be thus obtained." The district attorney's office followed this procedure in an investigation of the New York State Liquor Authority and obtained evidence leading to prosecution of Berger for conspiracy to bribe the chairman. Berger was convicted largely upon the evidence of the recordings, some of which were obtained by bugging the private offices of other conspirators. Berger appealed, claiming violation of the Fourth and Fifth Amendments. The Supreme Court reversed his conviction by a vote of 6-3. The contrariety of views is evidenced by six different opinions, three in the majority and three in dissent. Three points deserve attention.

First, the Court held that secret surveillance of private conversations is prohibited by the Fourth Amendment, if the electronic device is secreted inside the defendant's dwelling or office during a trespass. Most of the discussion would be equally applicable to a case in which there was no trespass. Justice Black alone stood on the *Olmstead* case, arguing that the Fourth Amendment bars only "searches and seizures" and protects only "houses, papers, and effects."[24] One does not "search" or "seize" a conversation, he said, and a conversation is not a house, paper, or effect. The opinion is a tribute to the Justice's consistency in giving effect to the belief that the Constitution must be applied as it was written and judges have no authority to keep it up to date by deviating from the literal meaning of the words even to apply it to modern devices unknown to the Framers. In my opinion the other justices had the better of the argument. The government's use of electronic bugs to penetrate the secrecy of the home or office is, in all significant respects, the same kind of official intrusion into privacy in search of evidence of wrongdoing as the Framers sought to outlaw by the Fourth Amendment. The interpretation of an on-going instrument that custom bars rewriting ought not to be limited to the specific applications with which the draftsmen were familiar, in disregard of the principle that lies behind them.

Second, the Court held that obtaining evidence by secret electronic surveillance of conversations would be constitutional provided that the government adhered to the search-warrant procedure contemplated by the Fourth Amendment. On this point, only Justice Douglas disagreed. With the full support of precedent he took the view that the Fourth Amendment bars all searches for mere evidence and limits the government to seizing contraband and the weapons or fruits of crime. This doctrine would have blocked any police use of electronic intrusions, assuming the Fourth Amendment to be applicable, because the only uses of a recording are to supply or lead one to evidence. The weight of professional opinion appears to be that, despite the precedents, the majority espoused the wiser rule. The old distinction contained more than a little hypocrisy. Frequently, the government's interest in the thing seized was purely technical, and the only purpose was to use it as evidence of guilt. Nor is there any interest save that of acquitting the guilty to be served by putting known, physical evidence of guilt beyond the government's power to procure.

The third branch of the *Berger* opinion reversed the conviction on the ground that the New York statute did not conform to the procedural requirements of the Fourth Amendment. The

Court found it defective because it failed to require the officers "to describe with particularity the conversation sought" and thus authorized them "to seize any and all conversations." An application describing only the person whose conversations were to be recorded was thought too general to satisfy the amendment. The opinion also criticized the statute for failure to require prompt execution of the warrant and cessation of the surveillance "once the conversation sought is seized"; the order authorizing surveillance was good for two months, 24 hours a day, and the time could be extended in the public interest. The Court's final objection was that the statute had "no requirement for notice as do conventional warrants nor does it overcome this defect by requiring some showing of special facts."

This branch of the *Berger* opinion has many extraordinary aspects—not the least of which is that its author was the father of an Attorney General who was even then engaged in sharp political controversy upon the same subject. There is no explanation of the Court's determination to judge the constitutionality of the New York statute on its face—a step theretofore reserved for restrictions upon freedom of expression. The normal course is to see whether what was done in the case at bar violated the constitutional rights of the defendant. Again, the *Berger* opinion leaves obscure the criteria it states for measuring the constitutionality of particular instances of electronic surveillance. Much of the language suggests that the order, which constitutes the search warrant, must limit the police to overhearing or recording a particular conversation. Since that can be done only when the police are able to identify the time, place, and participants in an expected conversation, and also to turn on their device for just the period necessary to hear it, the restriction would virtually eliminate the use of electronic devices in the detection of crime. Again, the suggestion that the statute was defective because there was no provision for notice of the execution of the warrant leaves several ambiguities. Must the notice be given in advance or after surveillance has ended? What "special facts" will excuse the omission of notice? Notice in advance is obviously self-defeating, and even in arrears it would alert the members of criminal rings to the closing in of police investigation.

Under the strictest interpretation it would be difficult to draw a statute satisfying the Court's reading of the requirements of the Fourth Amendment. Justice Clark's response was, "If that be true then the fruits of eavesdropping devices are barred under the Amendment." The answer seems inadequate. If the justices may interpret some of the words of the Fourth Amendment freely in order to protect those whose privacy may be invaded by scientific devices which the literal meaning does not prohibit, then the Court cannot consistently insist on reading other words literally in order to escape deciding the questions of policy involved in bringing the search warrant procedure into line with modern conditions.

The *Berger* case, although technically susceptible of limitation to situations in which there was a trespass, now sets the stage for congressional action. There is some reason to believe that F.B.I. Director Hoover previously placed such value upon uncontrolled discretion to use electronic devices in cases "involving the national security"—one wonders how broadly the term was defined—under the Jackson ruling that he opposed any new legislation. Since the *Berger* ruling seems to imply that any electronic surveillance is unconstitutional without a warrant, if there is time to secure one, continuation of the past practice will be of questionable constitutionality until a bill is enacted establishing a warrant procedure. Mr. Hoover's support would greatly improve the prospects for legislation.

In framing legislation it is easier to identify the considerations than to evaluate their relative importance. Electronic surveillance of conversations, on the telephone or otherwise, is a major invasion of .privacy affecting not only the suspect but many wholly innocent persons who converse with him about unrelated matters. On the other hand, such surveillance unquestionably has some value in law enforcement. No one denies this in instances affecting national security. How much value it has in other cases is obscure because those who are offended by the invasions of privacy tell us there is none and those who wish to legalize the practice testify to its great worth. Scarcely anyone seems to have found the truth coldly, as a matter of fact, because few detached observers have substantial information.

Under the best of circumstances it would be hard to know where to strike the balance or how to arrange an accommodation. The one clear point seems to be that the present situation is intolerable. Perhaps the best that can be done is to frame a temporary measure designed to strike a passable accommodation by effectively outlawing the clear abuses and regularizing the eavesdropping made permissible in such a way as to provide a factual foundation for subsequent reevaluation. Such a measure might embody these points:

(1) The Jackson ruling should be repudiated. The most worrisome invasions of privacy are in the eavesdropping and accumulation of materials in government files. If it is ever right to engage in the surveillance, it is no less right to use the information in the prosecution of wrongdoers.

(2) Electronic eavesdropping without a warrant, when there is time to procure one, should be prohibited. Under the *Berger* ruling this would seem to be a constitutional necessity, even in cases affecting the national security. The Department of Justice's cagily phrased abandonment of electronic eavesdropping

"for prosecutional purposes" is not enough to conform to the Fourth Amendment. Furthermore, requiring warrants is essential to removing the cloak of executive secrecy and bringing the practice under control.

(3) Authority to apply for warrants should be limited to the Attorney General and the Assistant Attorney General in charge of the Criminal Division and their State counterparts.

(4) "Warrants" should be obtainable only in connection with offenses against national security, organized racketeering, and other major crimes.

(5) Provision should be made for reports covering all instances of surveillance and the use of any information obtained. The problem, of course, is to obtain an accurate picture of the value and dangers of the practice without identifying the people affected.

Upon such a record of experience subsequent measures might be devised with considerably more understanding and less emotion than is possible today.

IV

The constitutional standards governing the use of confessions in criminal cases have been under debate and revision for nearly three decades. In 1966, in *Miranda* v. *Arizona*,[25] the Court endeavored to promulgate definitive rules.

Miranda had been arrested at his home and taken to the police station under suspicion of kidnapping and rape. He was questioned by two police officers. He was not told that he was entitled to have an attorney present, but at some point he apparently was informed that he need not make a statement and that anything he said might be used against him. After two hours of questioning, without threats or coercion, he signed a written statement confessing his guilt. The confession was admitted as evidence at the trial, and Miranda was convicted. The Supreme Court reversed upon the ground that the questioning and subsequent use of the confession as evidence violated the privilege against self-incrimination. Laying down broad rules for the guidance of the police and lower courts, the Supreme Court said that the prosecution may not use as evidence in a criminal case a statement resulting from police interrogation of a person in custody unless he has been warned of his right not to be questioned, of the danger that any statement may be used against him, and of his right to have an attorney present, either of his own retainer or appointed at public expense. The rights, moreover, even though waived initially, can be invoked at any time.

The *Miranda* decision has evoked both praise and criticism in roughly equal proportions, but I am more concerned here with what went into the decision than with its consequences. The ruling can hardly be explained by the words of the Constitution. The Fifth Amendment provides only that no person "shall be compelled in any criminal case to be a witness against himself." For more than a century and a half those words had never been held to require the presence of a lawyer during stationhouse interrogation. Some of the reasons for overturning the consistent line of precedents are in the Court's opinion. The rest can fairly be guessed.

In the first place, the Court was obviously troubled by fear that confessions were still being widely obtained by physical violence, threats, trickery, and other forms of overreaching the defendant's will. Beginning in the 1930's the Court reversed a long series of convictions where confessions had been obtained by torture, beatings, interrogation to the point of physical or psychological exhaustion, and isolation from lawyers, family, and friends.[26] New cases involving the same old police abuses continued to arise. Since relatively few such cases go to trial, the visible examples suggested that the secrecy of the stationhouse cloaked many other instances of the third degree in which the defendant was too poor or too cowed to make a defense, or in which the jury, figuring that a man would not confess if he were innocent, chose to believe the policemen's testimony rather than the defendant's account of the manner in which the police obtained his confession. If the third degree or subtler forms of coercing a confession were still prevalent after thirty or forty years of attempts to eliminate them by inquiry into the fact of coercion, case by case, had not the time come to establish a broader prophylactic rule that would bar all evidence of a confession unless some circumstance, such as the presence of the defendant's lawyer, gave assurance that the confession was voluntary?

A second factor in the thinking of some justices may have been the feeling that the time had come to eliminate some of the hypocrisy of our criminal procedure. We have long boasted that, in Anglo-American courts, every defendant is entitled to a lawyer to assist him in his defense; and that no man accused of crime need take the witness stand and subject himself to interrogation. At the same time we allowed prosecutors and police to interrogate defendants in the stationhouse in the presence of a stenographer, without the aid of a lawyer or the restraining influence of a judge. Police interrogators were trained in pyschological devices for obtaining confessions from reluctant suspects. Later, if a man confessed, the prosecutor would read into evidence at the trial either a transcript of the questioning or the narrative statement to which the answers were reduced. The boast that no man is required to testify against himself rings hollow next to the practice. If interrogation in the courtroom is different in any material respect from questioning in the station-house, read into evidence at the trial, the distinction lies in the fact that the stationhouse questioning is more susceptible of abuse.

A third element behind the *Miranda* ruling appears to be the egalitarianism that has become a dominant force in the evolution of our constitutional law. The broad egalitarianism stirred by the civil rights revolution had already found expression in criminal law in decisions requiring the State to offset inequalities of wealth by paying for a lawyer for the defendant[27] and furnishing a stenographic transcript for appeal.[28] Who were the defendants who were led into giving confessions in police stations? Not the well-to-do, who could procure a lawyer immediately. Not the experienced criminal, who knew enough to keep silent until his mouthpiece arrived. More often than not those who confessed in the police station would be the poor and ignorant, the friendless and frightened, or the young and weak. Should not society be required to do what it could to put them on an equality with the more fortunate, or at least to stop taking advantage of their situation?

Broader forces undoubtedly contributed to the *Miranda* decision, as they have influenced the general trend of constitutional development in criminal law. The law is feeling the impact of the newer sciences. As mentioned in the first lecture, the doubts which psychologists raise concerning freedom of the will breed skepticism of the very notions of guilt and punishment. Much of our criminal law is based upon the premise that antisocial conduct can be deterred by fear of punishment, but many observers have come to question the predicate in the face of the social, economic, and psychological causes of crime. Most prison systems appear to breed more criminals than they cure.

One wonders whether respect for, and therefore observance of, law is better secured by the tough cop and frequent convictions, however obtained, or by requiring law enforcement officials to observe practices earning respect for their fairness. We are woefully ignorant upon all such questions, as we are about the anatomy of crime. I do not mean to imply that the majority of the Court is committed to any view, but the doubts arising from awareness of ignorance, when they replace once accepted verities, are likely to influence the course of decision.

The active intervention of the Warren Court into the administration of criminal justice followed State defaults, both legislative and judicial. It would have been better if the States had themselves reformed their criminal procedure by providing counsel for all indigent defendants at public expense, but the simple fact is that a minority of States failed to act despite a long period of warning. For years it was plain that State and local police often resorted to unlawful searches and seizures, but the local courts continued to offer incentives for misconduct by receiving the fruits of the illegality as evidence without adopting other measures to restrain the officials from invading constitutional rights. The problem of coerced confessions is another example. Of course, not all the business of government is constitutional law, but if one arm of government cannot or will not solve an insistent problem, the pressure falls upon another. This has been a major factor in the Supreme Court's activity in the field of criminal law.

V

If one may measure "activism" by the overruling of settled precedents and the establishment of new constitutional doctrines, the Warren Court has been extraordinarily "activist" in the field of criminal procedure. If Winston Churchill was right in saying that "the quality of a nation's civilization can be largely measured by the methods it uses in the enforcement of its criminal law," then the activism of the Warren Court has enabled our civilization to give a vastly better account of itself. There is room for honest debate as to whether such decisions as *Miranda* go too far in correcting the acknowledged evil. A number of dissenting opinions and even some opinions of the Court seem to slide off into sentimentality or run libertarian dogma into the ground at the expense of the substance of liberty, as happened when the Court held that search warrants must be obtained for routine fire or health inspections but then watered down the showing required for a warrant until the requirement would be little more than red tape.[29] Despite occasional excesses the net effect has been extraordinarily important reform in the administration of criminal justice, in the States where reform was most needed, within an unusually short span of time.

Nor should the consequences be measured solely in terms of legal doctrine. The establishment of a constitutional requirement for the appointment of counsel in all criminal cases, for example, set in motion countless local reforms because the activity of counsel brought to the attention of judges practices that had escaped their notice or which they had let slide, such as confining offenders for long periods without arraignment or advice about their legal rights. The spirit engendered by the decisions supplied much of the stimulus for broader undertakings such as the Attorney General's Conference on Bail, the Attorney General's Conference on the Provision of Legal Services to the Indigent, and the work of the President's Commission on Law Enforcement and the Administration of Justice.

The costs of the Court's activism must be reckoned in long-range institutional terms. The rapidity of the doctrinal changes and the readiness of a bare numerical majority of the justices to overturn recent precedents immediately upon a change in the membership of the Court do no service to the ideal of law as something distinct from the arbitrary preferences of individuals. Yet misgivings on this score should be tempered by the realization that many of the changes have roots in prior decisions. The constitutional rights of the defendant in a federal trial are stated with some degree of specificity, and the Court had long been evolving the doctrines necessary for their implementation. By the doctrine of selective incorporation those guarantees have now been applied to the States. The decisions brought sharp changes in some States, for they had applied much looser standards, but the rationale is necessarily self-limiting. Once the federal rights are carried over to the States the pace of change may be slowed.

The gravest questions are raised by the radical revision of the structure of government that results from shifting the ultimate judicial responsibility for the administration of criminal justice from the States to the Nation — a point the majority refuses to discuss despite Justice Harlan's dissents.[30] Under the older view of due process a criminal prosecution seldom raised questions of constitutional law. Today constitutional law affects innumerable aspects of criminal cases from investigation to sentence, and recent decisions suggest that the Court is ready to deal with more and more details.[31] The judgments of the State courts of last resort are thus subject not only to reversal by the Supreme Court of the United States on certiorari but also, under the rule allowing the use of federal habeas corpus to review constitutional questions, to scrutiny by a federal district judge, the federal court of appeals, and again the Supreme Court. Even if the possibility of injustice makes so much judicial review a wise allocation of resources, one wonders about the consequences of the delay in reaching a truly final decision in the case of defendants with the funds and perseverance to exhaust every conceivable remedy. Moreover, men of ability may find that positions on State courts of last resort become less attractive if they are reduced to way stations on the route to ultimate constitutional review; and the State judges may feel less and less inclined to exercise responsibility for continuing improvement in the administration of criminal justice. It is far from clear that we can wisely look to the impulse of constitutional adjudication for continuing reform.

In the New York eavesdropping case Justice Harlan protested his colleagues' new contrivance of constitutional rights "without apparent concern for the empirical process that goes with legislative reform."[32] If the apparent lack of concern is real, then the institutional changes associated with reform by constitutional adjudication could indeed tend to freeze a particular set of preconceptions into permanence at a time when the public concern about crime in the streets and the work of the President's Commission may stimulate new investigations enormously increasing our understanding of the practical impact of sundry rules of criminal procedure. I am more inclined to believe that the Court is simply filling a void, and that the present use of constitutional law will not bar careful legislation in the future. Generally speaking, the administration of criminal justice has thus far been the special responsibility of the judicial branch on both the State and federal level. The Supreme Court, in imposing changes, has not yet disturbed the processes of representative self-government.

Perhaps we may glean some hint of the future from a passage in the Chief Justice's opinion in the *Miranda* case where he carefully left room for movement by emphasizing that the procedural safeguards the opinion requires are applicable "unless other fully effective means are devised to inform accused persons of their right of silence and to assure a continuous opportunity to exercise it." Later he declared that "Congress and the States are free to develop their own safeguards" for the privilege against self-incrimination during questioning by the police.[33]

The Constitution bars some changes in criminal procedure, however fair and however soundly based on empirical investigation they may be. The right to jury trial, for example, limits the functions that can be delegated to a board of experts, and the privilege against self-incrimination bars accusatorial investigation. The Court would doubtless give short shrift to legislative attempts to authorize the very same police practices which it has recently proscribed unless the legislation was based upon new data. Within such limits, however, nothing in the Court's opinions is inhospitable to legislative action rooted in careful investigation, even if it involves some qualification of the doctrines announced in recent cases. Indeed, one of the chief benefits flowing from the recent decisions may be the stimulus they have given to more empirical channels of study and reform.

5   Political Democracy:
Speech and Association

THE WARREN COURT, more than any of its predecessors, has been influenced by an intensely conscious sense of judicial responsibility for the open and democratic operation of the political system, at least so far as it can be influenced by law. The concern is evident in two groups of cases. The recent decisions dealing with the workings of democracy in the development of political opinion — the flow of information, criticism and debate, voluntary association, demonstrations and dissent — strengthen and extend an inherited constitutional tradition, but the vision from which they flow encompasses greater turbulence and faster changes in society than the intellectual liberalism of the eighteenth and nineteenth centuries. These cases are discussed in the present lecture. The final lecture deals with the assertion of constitutional control over such aspects of the electoral process as the apportionment of legislative representatives and eligibility to vote. Direct precedent was lacking for that judicial venture.

I

    Concern for the democratic operation of the political system is closely related to the constitutional protection of individual liberty. Suppression of speech is an affront to the human personality because the man burdened with an idea feels a need to express it. Discussion of matters of governmental concern is also indispensable to the operation of representative self-government.

Even in the beginning James Madison foresaw a special role for the Supreme Court in enforcing the Bill of Rights. During the debates in Congress he argued that if these rights were incorporated into the Constitution, "independent tribunals of justice will consider themselves in a peculiar manner the guardians of those rights; they will be an impenetrable bulwark against every assumption of power in the Legislative or Executive."[1]

The flowering of this judicial function, in the area of political liberties, was reserved for an age in which the increasing interdependence and complexity of all parts of human society multiplied and magnified governmental activities. The First Amendment stood as a warning to the Congress, but as late as 1922 the Court declared, "neither the Fourteenth Amendment nor any other provision of the Constitution of the United States imposes upon the States any restrictions about 'freedom of speech.'"[2] Within a decade the First Amendment had been incorporated into the Fourteenth by judicial interpretation. Today the enforcement of the First Amendment against the States occupies a substantial part of the docket.

The doctrinal change occurred about the same time as the Court began to reject judicial use of the due process clause to invalidate social and economic legislation. The Jeffersonian philosophy of legislative supremacy was ascendant. The Court was liberally invoking both the principle of deference to legislative judgments and the presumption of constitutionality which holds that a statute will not be invalidated upon judicial review if any rationally conceivable state of facts would sustain it. In cases under the First Amendment, the Court seemed to give little weight to legislative judgments upon the ground that First Amendment freedoms hold a preferred position. Many thoughtful persons, however, Learned Hand and Felix Frankfurter among them, found it inconsistent to follow the legislative-supremacy approach in sustaining social and economic measures and then to turn around and substitute judicial findings and values for the conclusions of elected representatives in dealing with restraints upon speech or association. The supposed dichotomy between "personal rights" and "property rights" left them unpersuaded because, as Learned Hand used to say, "No one will ever tell me why holding property is not a personal liberty."

In a famous footnote in the *Carolene Products* case,[3] Justice Stone suggested a rationalization which puts the weight upon the protection of self-government: "It is unnecessary to consider now whether legislation which restricts those political processes which can ordinarily be expected to bring about repeal of undesirable legislation, is to be subjected to more exacting judicial scrutiny under the general prohibitions of the Fourteenth Amendment than are most other types of legislation." The implication is this: When the political channels of debate and change are open, one may answer a challenge to the legislative results of self-government that alleges their unfairness or folly, by saying that relief should be sought in the legislatures and among the people under the principle of majority rule because anything else would be a denial of self-government. The case is different when access to the political process is closed or its operation is distorted by the challenged legislation. Then relief must come from the outside because the measure itself raises improper obstacles to political correction.

Justice Stone's suggestion is not often cited nowadays — but it furnishes the strongest support for the Court's sensitivity to claims of freedom of speech, association, and assembly. Even more important, it encourages raising constitutional (and therefore judicial) safeguards against other statutes or practices closing or distorting the processes of democratic government. The Reapportionment Cases to be discussed in the next chapter are a prime illustration.

II

Self-government, as the Warren Court sees it, begins with lively, indeed lusty and uninhibited, debate over issues, candidates for office, and the conduct of public officials. Dr. Alexander Meiklejohn argued that whereas other constitutional immunities are restrictions protecting the citizen against abuse of the powers delegated to government by the people, the guarantees of freedom of speech and the press are measures adopted by the people as the ultimate rulers to withhold all power over those subjects from their legislative and executive agents. The Court adopted something very like this view of the absolute protection to be accorded political debate when Justice Brennan wrote for the Court that "speech concerning public affairs is more than self-expression; it is the essence of self-government."[4] In a subsequent lecture Justice Brennan acknowledged the indebtedness to Dr. Meiklejohn.[5]

The theory is part of a substantial change in constitutional doctrine. Throughout our history, civil damages and sometimes criminal sentences have been imposed under the law of libel for publishing false statements of fact about government officials. In 1960 the *New York Times* published an advertisement attacking the conduct of the police during civil rights demonstrations in Montgomery. The advertisement contained minor misstatements such as that the police had "ringed" the Alabama State College Campus when in fact they were merely deployed near the campus in large numbers. An Alabama jury awarded the Montgomery Commissioner of Public Affairs $500,000 for actual and punitive damages. The Supreme Court unanimously reversed, holding that the First Amendment bars a public official from recovering damages for a defamatory falsehood relating to his official conduct unless the statement was made with knowledge that it was false or with reckless disregard of whether it was true or false. Behind the rule lies the judgment that any risk of injury to private reputations resulting from such a rule is outweighed by the benefits to democratic self-government that flow from encouraging public debate about official conduct uninhibited by fear of liability if statements made in honest error turn out to be false. The *New York Times* case itself was a dramatic reminder of the extent to which the overhanging threat of huge judgments for libel might discourage open discussion of vital issues in sections of the country where the local media are closed and popular feeling runs high against criticism of the established order.

The reasoning also seems to foreshadow the modification of precedents that apply the "clear and present danger" test in such a way as to punish men for the advocacy of ideas which create a risk, albeit remote, of the violent overthrow of the government.[6] So long as ideas of importance in self-government are held to be reserved from control by government, restrictions will have to be limited to considerations of time, place, and possibly the medium of utterance.

The *New York Times* doctrine has won general and enthusiastic approval, both as it repudiates the old doctrines of seditious libel and as it relates the preferred position of speech to the ideal of popular self-government. Without depreciating the main accomplishment, one may suggest that a good deal more is required for the full discharge of the Supreme Court's function. Fundamental human interests often conflict with one another, so that too enthusiastic pursuit of one desideratum sacrifices another. The interest in freedom of expression, for example, sometimes collides with an interest in privacy unbroken by the intrusions of the press. Nor is the interest in freedom of expression necessarily an integer. The concept has one justification as applied to discussion of the conduct of public officials and quite another, if any, as applied to private individuals in matters without "governing importance." Here the proper judicial task may be one of differentiation and accommodation rather than the pursuit of ever more "breathing space" for the media of expression.

In our federal system the creation of a new constitutional privilege may also require corollary rules weaving it into the complex relationships between State and federal law and between State and federal courts. Prior to the *New York Times* case the rules governing liability for injury to reputation, invasion of privacy, and like interference with interests of personality had always been an exclusive province of the States. The effect of the new doctrine is thus to "nationalize" a significant segment of this body of law. Unless the Supreme Court of the United States is to act as if it were the court of first instance or a State court of last resort, it must attend to the technical and subtle relation between the State law governing the basic protection accorded interests of personality and the federal rules protecting freedom of expression.

Time, Inc. v. *Hill*[7] illustrates the difficulties. On September 11, 1952, three escaped convicts entered the Hills' home in suburban Philadelphia and held the parents and five children captive for nineteen hours. Later the convicts left. Two were shot by the police, and one was recaptured. The incident became a front-page story. Shortly thereafter the Hills moved to Connecticut and discouraged all efforts to prolong the publicity. Their connection with the incident was forgotten.

Six months after the incident James Hayes' novel *The Desperate Hours* was published. It depicted the experience of a family of four held captive by escaped convicts, but this family, unlike the Hills, suffered violence in the invasion. Apparently nothing was done to connect either the Hills or the original incident with the book. In February 1955, about two and a half years after the original incident, the book was made into a play and the play was widely publicized in *Life* magazine under the caption "True Crime Inspires Tense Play." The account was inaccurate. There were photographs of the actors in the Hills' original Philadelphia house depicting fictitious scenes of violence and brutality.

The Hills, who had moved and put the incident with its attendant notoriety behind them, brought suit under New York's so-called "right-to-privacy" statute. The vicissitudes of legislative draftsmanship and judicial interpretation had given the statute a strange quirk. Although one might think that the gist of the wrong was *Life's* dredging up a forgotten incident in the life of a quiet family for the sake of selling magazines — an equal injury to the interest in privacy whether the account was true or false — the New York law granted relief only if the published account was fictionalized, *i.e.,* contained substantial errors. The issue was simply one of substantial truth or falsity; it was irrelevant whether the misstatements were innocent, negligent, reckless, or intentional. In the *Hill* case the jury found that the account was false and originally awarded $50,000 compensatory and $25,000 punitive damages.

The Supreme Court of the United States reversed the judg-ment. Three justices concluded that "the constitutional protec-tions for speech and press preclude the application of the New York statute to redress false reports of matters of public interest in the absence of proof that the defendant published the report with knowledge of its falsity or in reckless disregard of the truth."[8] There were other opinions but apparently all the justices agreed that the First Amendment gave *Life* a constitutional privilege to thrust the Hills back into unwanted limelight by a false dramatization of their forgotten plight, unless the Hills could prove that there was something blameworthy in the errors. The dispute was over whether the privilege should be still broader.

One may profitably compare *Time, Inc.* v. *Hill* with a case decided some years ago in California.[9] A movie studio released a picture called *The Red Kimono,* which described the life of a former prostitute who had been tried and acquitted for murder eight years before. The picture used the prostitute's real name and stressed its faithfulness to actual events; apparently the advertising also revealed the erstwhile prostitute's current mar-ried name and identity even though she had reformed, married, and lived a quiet and secluded life for seven years, with a buried past. The California District Court of Appeals held that upon those facts the woman had a right of action for invasion of her privacy. Does *Time, Inc.* v. *Hill* mean that today the producer of the motion picture would have a constitutional defense? The two cases are factually indistinguishable, save that the suffering inflicted by reviving the housewife's bygone past is somewhat more obvious than the Hills' suffering.

Justice Brennan, who wrote the principal opinion in *Hill,* would probably reply that the question was left open. Quite early in the opinion he observed, "Constitutional questions which might arise if truth were not a defense are therefore of no concern."[10] Justice Harlan also stressed the narrowness of the problem: in his view the *Hill* case was not privacy litigation in its truest sense, because the entire case had been conducted, under the law of New York, upon the theory that an article of the same type, but unfictionalized, could have been published without liability. But it would be difficult to square allowing the girl in the red kimono a right of action with the denial of recovery to the Hills. If the girl had sufficient interest in privacy to recover damages for the injury done by true publicity about her lurid past, then surely she had enough interest in privacy to recover damages for false publicity, regardless of whether the falsity resulted from negligence, recklessness, or malice. Conversely, if the public interest in knowledge of dramatic events is sufficient to override the interest in privacy when the account is false, it must be sufficient to override the interest when the account is accurate. If, as *Hill* seems to hold, the girl in the red kimono could not recover from the false publicity, *a fortiori* she could not recover for the true.

The logic suggests that the Court must either recant *Hill* or else acknowledge that it gave Brandeis' great right of privacy a constitutional burial so quiet as to deny its demise. It is ironic that the deed should have been done by a Court which has repeatedly quoted Brandeis' plea while elevating privacy to a constitutional right against governmental intrusions.[11] The risks from invasion by the press are much the greater. The justification seems the less.

The avenue of escape suggested by Justices Brennan and Harlan—that the constitutional principles applicable to defamation applied in the *Hill* case and those dealing with the protection of privacy were irrelevant because New York was securing an interest in reputation—encounters three difficulties. First, the dichotomy is artificial. New York could just as accurately be said to have been protecting the Hills' interest in privacy: in fact the New York rule protects both interests, because a requirement of adherence to the truth, which is seldom as dramatic as fiction, makes it less likely that the press will want to invade the privacy of quiet people. Second, drawing the distinction would result in such incongruities as allowing protection against fictionalized invasions of privacy in California but not in New York even though all the facts, except the locale, were identical. Variations in State law are familiar but it would be extraordinary to find that the Constitution gives a defense in one State that it withholds upon identical facts in another. Third, the divergent rulings would result in making constitutional rights turn not upon what was done to the plaintiff by the defendant nor upon what judgment the state court rendered, but rather upon what the State court said in its opinion and in related cases by way of explanation. It is this last aspect of the matter which leads me to suggest that the Court was not sufficiently attentive to the complexities of introducing a new constitutional privilege into an area generally governed by State law.

Perhaps these difficulties will prove less important than they seem. One would wish, however, that the *Hill* opinions contained more evidence of the Court's addressing itself to the consequences of its enthusiasm for protecting the press against the individuals whom it injures. The prevailing opinion contains no real discussion of why the Constitution should be held to give the press a privilege to subject the Hills to false publicity despite their genuine and apparently successful retreat into privacy. The *New York Times* decision was put squarely upon the ground that uninhibited discussion of such matters as the conduct of the police toward civil rights demonstrations was essential to self-government. In *Hill* we are told, "The guarantees for speech and press are not the preserve of political expression or comment upon public affairs, essential as those are to healthy government . . . We have no doubt that the subject of the *Life* article, the opening of a new play linked to an actual incident, is a matter of public interest."[12]

That the public would be interested in hearing about the Hills' misadventure may be admitted: doubtless their new neighborhood buzzed with discussion. Whether there was enough public value in the disclosure to justify the affront to the Hills is quite a different question. It is not answered by asserting that it is enough to "pick up any newspaper or magazine to comprehend the vast range of published matter which exposes persons to public view, both private citizens and public officials"; for this amounts to saying that anything the press chooses to publish has such overriding importance that privacy must yield. Similarly, to say that a "broadly defined freedom of the press assures the maintenance of our political system and an open society" is not an adequate answer to the suggestion that any public value in linking a current play to an actual incident in the life of an identified person is insufficient to justify negligent falsification. The needs of the political system support only comment upon public issues and political affairs. The reference to an "open society," in this context, is opaque.

The *New York Times* and *Hill* cases, taken together, suggest that the Court was more successful in making a bold thrust forward than in working out the corollaries necessary to integrate the principle into a complex legal system. Yet it is important to keep our perspective. The right to privacy had proved scarcely viable in a society whose tone is set by advertising, publicity, and noise. The final discard of the doctrine of seditious libel and the adoption of the Meiklejohn theory, when properly refined, may prove major contributions to the operation of democratic government.

III

Freedom of political association must rank close to liberty of expression in a large heavily populated country, where group organization is essential to effective political action. The question seldom arose in earlier periods, but in *NAACP* v. *Alabama*[13] and *Bates* v. *Little Rock*[14] the present Court sustained the right of an association to withhold its membership lists from official scrutiny, and of a school teacher to withhold knowledge of her associations, where the State demonstrated no need for the information and where publication of memberships was very likely to result in social and economic reprisals and perhaps even physical violence.

In theory, a right of secret association is not easily reconciled with a philosophy that justifies freedom of speech by the importance of competition in the marketplace of ideas. The identity, experience, reputation, and motivation of the sponsors of an idea are relevant to its evaluation. In practice, however, the community probably must assure far-out groups some degree of secrecy lest they perish before the seeds they sow can germinate. This necessity also supports the decisions curtailing legislative investigations into allegedly "subversive activities" of individuals and invalidating laws designed to bar "subversives" from public employment. The latest example is the invalidation of New York's Feinburg law,[15] the constitutionality of which had been upheld earlier in *Adler* v. *Board of Education*.[16]

Constitutional protection for the far-out groups seeking to overthrow the established order rests upon the vision of a society open to endless self-renewal. Only opinions which are so extreme as to frighten right-minded people are likely to be suppressed by governmental action, but history reveals that it is the small bands of heretics, like the early Christians and the Abolitionists, who stimulate the most important changes in civilization. Perhaps heretics are very seldom right, but their value upon those rare occasions is too great to trust the power to separate falsehood from truth to government officials. In protecting heretics the Court is protecting the opportunity for progress.

IV

The preservation of an open and changing society requires more than freedom for extremists to organize and speak their ideas. They must find effective vehicles for expression. Justice Douglas has eloquently described their difficulties in making themselves audible: "Conventional methods of petitioning may be, and often have been, shut off to large groups of our citizens. Legislators may turn deaf ears; formal complaints may be routed endlessly through a bureaucratic maze; courts may let the wheels of justice grind very slowly. Those who do not control television and radio, those who cannot afford to advertise in newspapers or circulate elaborate pamphlets may have only a more limited type of access to public officials." Justice Douglas concluded: "Their methods should not be condemned as tactics of obstruction and harassment as long as the assembly and petition are peaceable, as these were."[17]

For the civil rights movement the vehicles of expression became the sit-in, picketing, marches, and mass demonstrations, often at State capitols, jails, and courthouses. Their success led to protests against the United States' involvement in Viet Nam in the form of draft-card burning, sit-ins in the offices of local Selective Service Boards, mass obstruction of recruiting, and a massive march on the Pentagon. Such techniques of dissent are often loosely lumped together as civil disobedience. Most of them have in common a capacity for attracting wide attention, an element of risk to the demonstrator evidencing the strength of his conviction, and the defiance of restrictions imposed by official representatives of the established order. All of them involve more than the oral or written dissemination of ideas because they involve specific forms of expression at a particular time and place.

Cox v. *Louisiana*[18] illustrates one approach of the Warren Court, to political demonstrations. Two thousand students left the campus of Southern University, a Negro college in Baton Rouge, and assembled at a site two and a half blocks from the courthouse where twenty-three of their fellow students were in jail charged with illegally picketing segregated lunch counters. The Rev. B. Elton Cox planned to lead the assembly on a march to the courthouse to protest both the specific arrests and the broader evil of segregation. Police officials objected to any assembly, but when the demonstrators began the march the chief of police told Cox only that he must confine the demonstration to the west side of the street, across from the courthouse. The demonstrators were orderly. They lined the sidewalk five deep, but the street was not blocked. They sang *God Bless America* and *We Shall Overcome*. The students in jail joined the singing. Cox then delivered a speech which he concluded by urging the demonstrators to go to the segregated lunch counters and demand service. At this point the sheriff ordered the demonstrators to disperse; they refused and tear gas shells were exploded. The next day Cox was arrested. Later he was convicted of breach of the peace under a Louisiana statute punishing "whoever with intent to provoke a breach of the peace or under circumstances such that a breach of the peace may be occasioned thereby . . . crowds . . . upon a public sidewalk . . ."

The Supreme Court of the United States reversed the conviction, by a 5-4 vote, in an opinion with two significant aspects. First, the Court rejected the argument that the street demonstration should be equated to speech: "We emphatically reject the notion that the First and Fourteenth Amendments afford the same kind of freedom to those who would communicate ideas by conduct such as patrolling, marching, and picketing on streets and highways ... as to those who communicate ideas by pure speech ..." Second, the Court held the statute void for "overbreadth" under the First and Fourteenth Amendments, upon this reasoning: the words making it unlawful to crowd upon a public sidewalk "under circumstances such that a breach of the peace may be occasioned thereby" could be read by the State authorities to allow persons to be punished merely for expressing unpopular views; such an application would be unconstitutional because the State has a duty to preserve the peace, where it can, by suppressing violence directed against the expression of unpopular views instead of suppressing their expression; where a statute restricting speech in general terms is unconstitutional as written, the courts will not rewrite it by excising the unconstitutional application and saving whatever is constitutional — partly because the failure of the statute to give express warning of the line between the legal and illegal renders it void for vagueness, partly because the courts cannot tell where the legislature would have drawn the line, and partly because the very existence of a law with uncertain boundaries discourages constitutionally protected speech. Consequently, Cox's conviction was reversed even though the State might have been permitted to punish the very same conduct under a statute properly drafted.

One of the dilemmas of constitutional adjudication lies in the need to perform the duty of judicial review without merely second-guessing the legislature in situations where both the wisdom and constitutionality of a statute depend upon an appraisal of the same conflicting interests. In the 1920's, for example, the power of a legislature to engage in price regulation was said to depend upon whether the public interest served by the controls was sufficient to outweigh the private interest in liberty of contract. When the legislature enacted the regulation, it struck one balance. When the Court invalidated it as unconstitutional, the justices struck another. The problem is partly analogous to this when government officials attempt to bar a parade or other demonstration which blocks the streets and sidewalks, causes disturbance, and interferes with the activities of others. Since such a demonstration is not pure speech but speech entwined with conduct, both the wisdom of restriction and the constitutional power to impose it depend upon the balance struck between the need for the restriction and the interest in political expression. Although the formula applied to the regulation of property and business conduct precludes substituting the Court's judgment for the legislature's, at least where the legislature's evaluation may be thought rational, the preferred position accorded freedom of expression encourages substitution to a much greater degree.

It is all the more significant, therefore, that the decisions of the Warren Court dealing with demonstrations have usually avoided holding that the legislature had no power to impose a restriction; rather they have rested upon such grounds as that the statute was broader than required to meet the evil;[19] or was unconstitutionally vague in its prohibitions;[20] or delegated untrammeled power to a petty official;[21] or, as in *Cox*, was so broad as to forbid other constitutionally protected conduct without indicating how much of the prohibition, if all were invalid, the legislature would wish to impose.[22] The tests are stricter than in dealing with the regulation of business activity. The decisions reflect substantive as well as procedural concern for liberty of expression. The same results might have been reached even if the legislature had specifically condemned the exact conduct involved in the particular cases. Still, taking the current approach at face value, it achieves four purposes:

(a) it avoids direct conflict with the legislature insofar as possible;

(b) it denies local prosecutors and other minor functionaries the power to decide what ideas may be expressed, or where, when, and how they shall find expression, because such power, whether exercised under a licensing act or by selective application of a loosely defined crime (such as breach of the peace) is all too likely to become a weapon against small and unpopular minorities;

(c) it forces the legislature to face up to the hard and specific choices between particular forms of expression and competing social or private interests; and

(d) it safeguards the expression of ideas, even though enmeshed in conduct subject to regulation, in the absence of an exact legislative interdiction.

The desire to force the entire body to face up to making the concrete choices in exercising legislative authority in the area of political activities, coupled with reluctance to limit legislative power, seemingly underlies a number of decisions reversing convictions for contempt of Congress upon the ground that the congressional committees investigating subversive activities had not obtained proper authorization or had failed to follow their own rules of procedure.[23]

The two groups of cases, taken together, suggest that the weight of opinion in the Court is reluctant to upset a careful legislative evaluation of conflicting interests even in some areas of expression.

V

The extent of the citizen's right to demonstration in defiance of local authority next came before the Court in *Brown* v. *Louisiana.*[24] Five young Negroes went to a small branch public library in Louisiana in order to protest the policy of racial segregation. They entered, requested a book, and were informed that the branch did not have it but could obtain it for them from the State capitol. The Negroes refused to leave, and stayed even after the sheriff requested. They were arrested and convicted of breach of the peace under a Louisiana statute punishing those who congregate in a public building with intent to provoke a breach of the peace, or under circumstances such that a breach of the peace may be occasioned, and then refuse to disperse when ordered by a law enforcement officer. The Supreme Court reversed the convictions by a 5-4 vote, although the majority was badly split as to the reason. Justice White concluded that whites would not have been prosecuted under identical circumstances; on that supposition, the convictions were flagrant violations of the equal protection clause of the Fourteenth Amendment. Justice Brennan argued that the statute was unconstitutional under *Cox* v. *Louisiana,* in an opinion which succumbs to the temptation of conjuring up fanciful unconstitutional applications of a statute which will render the whole void for overbreadth, thus escaping the question whether the defendants' conduct was protected by the First Amendment. Seven justices squarely faced the latter question. The Chief Justice and Justices Douglas and Fortas (who together with Justices Brennan and White made a majority for reversal) held that the sit-in at the segregated library, even after the demonstrators had been given the full service its limited facilities offered, was protected by the constitutional guarantees of freedom of speech and assembly.

Later the full Court decided this issue, in principle, in *Adder-*

ly v. *Florida*,[25] the first Supreme Court decision which civil rights demonstrators have lost on the merits. The petitioners were college students who assembled at Florida A. & M. and marched to the county jail to conduct a demonstration protesting segregation policies and particularly the imprisonment of a number of their fellows who had been arrested for attempting to desegregate local theaters. About two hundred demonstrators entered into a service driveway and grassy area which were not normally open to the public. The crowd was peaceful. It did nothing to break into the jail or to interfere with normal activities, except as the crowd may have caused some inconvenience. The demonstrators sang songs. After a short time the sheriff notified them that they were trespassing and that unless they left within ten minutes they would be arrested. Some left; others stayed. Some who stayed said that they wanted to be arrested. One hundred seven demonstrators were arrested for criminal trespass and convicted in the Florida courts. The Supreme Court of the United States affirmed the convictions. Speaking through Justice Black, the Court concluded that petitioners had not been deprived of their rights to freedom of speech, press, assembly, or petition, because a "State, no less than a private owner of property, has power to preserve the property under its control for the use to which it is lawfully dedicated."

Justice Douglas' dissenting opinion, quoted earlier, was joined by the Chief Justice and Justices Brennan and Fortas. After a powerful plea for the need to permit unconventional forms of expression that may reach the public conscience despite the barriers to use of conventional mass media, Justice Douglas argued that where there was neither violence nor other significant interference with customary activities, the bare proprietary interest of the State was insufficient to justify the suppression of what the demonstrators found their more effective vehicle for protesting racial oppression.

One wonders whether either opinion gets to the root of the issue. The very characteristics that gave the demonstration at the jail house special claims to constitutional protection also raised special reasons for permitting the State to restrict this form of expression.

A demonstration at the jail house was the most effective method by which Florida A. & M. students could express their grievance against the arrest of their fellows, without resort to violence. Their fellows had, at worst, committed minor infractions by demonstrating against racial segregation in public places. The students did not ordinarily have access to the most effective means of mass communications. The establishment, in Florida, was hardly likely to publicize their argument. Very few people, not already zealous in the movement, would interrupt normal activities to listen to their speeches or read their leaflets. The demonstration was effective not merely because it focused the widest publicity upon the wrong but also because it challenged the establishment to the point of inviting arrest, thus demonstrating a courage and depth of conviction that might embolden others to throw off the bonds by which the community perpetuated racial injustice. The technique was effective also because it put the authorities in a dilemma; either they must jail students for peacefully protesting official support for segregation, which would put the authorities in a shockingly immoral position, or else they must tolerate a mass demonstration in a place and under circumstances where the defiance of authority was unmistakable.

But such a demonstration at such a place presents peculiar danger of the outbreak of violence. Law enforcement officials and other persons hostile to the demonstrators are unlikely to acquiesce calmly in a flaunted challenge to their authority. At best, fighting words may be uttered or the demonstrators' antagonists may resort to similar "nonviolent action" colliding with the demonstrators' activities and creating a tinder box of tension. Those charged with keeping order could hardly be expected to know who struck the spark, especially where the demonstrators were consciously seeking martyrdom. Such a demonstration, moreover, depends upon its own lawlessness to make it effective: if government officials, the press, and the public all knew that there was a constitutional right to demonstrate in the jail yard—if no one objected—the demonstration would have attracted no greater attention than a meeting in a park.

So long as civil rights demonstrators were violating unconstitutional Jim Crow laws, as in the freedom rides and possibly in the lunch counter sit-ins—so long as the restrictions upon marches and picketing were imposed under local ordinances void for vagueness or the excessive delegation of censorial power—the challenge to established local authority was only a superficial form of civil disobedience. One may disregard with legal impunity the commands of civil authorities (but not of a court) if what the authorities forbid is in truth only the exercise of a privilege guaranteed by the United States Constitution. Such action involves no civil disobedience—no violation of law in the ultimate sense—because the only orders that are violated, being unconstitutional, are not law. There is no constitutional right of civil disobedience to an otherwise valid law.

Although the moral question may sometimes be different, it is regrettable that so many of those now engaged in protests have failed to observe this elementary distinction. Not one of the great events in the civil rights movement involved Negroes' disobedience of an admittedly valid law—not Tuscaloosa in 1956, Little Rock in 1957, the Freedom Rides in 1961, Oxford in 1962, nor even Selma in 1965, where Dr. King made public statements seeming to suggest disobedience yet in the end acted on the advice of lawyers in the good-faith belief that he was not in contempt of the court. The only true civil disobedience of importance in the civil rights struggle was on the part of Governors Barnett and Wallace when, asserting what they believed was a moral principle, they refused to desegregate State schools in compliance with the final orders of the federal courts. Similarly, I can recall no instance in which civil rights demonstrators used the sheer weight of numbers "nonviolently" to obstruct the lawful activities of others, to suppress argument, or in an effort to impose their views upon the community by sheer harassment.

Perhaps there is sometimes a moral right of revolution even in a society as open as ours to political reform, but I do not see how a free society can survive if "nonviolent" harassment of others and violation of law replace reason and civility as methods of resolving questions of public policy whenever one side or the other sees the difference as a moral issue. Power alone will ensure neither individual liberty nor the opportunity for each generation to remake society, if it can, without violent revolution. Law, so far as history reveals, is the only substitute for power; and law, as a restraint of power, depends upon voluntary compliance with the final decisions reached by constitutional processes. The man who is willing to deny the force of law, in order to impose his views upon society, must be peculiarly arrogant or extremely shortsighted.

6   Political Democracy: Voting Rights
and Legislative Apportionment

THE DOCTRINE OF JUDICIAL REVIEW vests in the Supreme Court of the United States a large measure of responsibility for the operation of our political system, not only in terms of the distribution of governmental power but also in keeping open the channels of political debate. Prior to 1960, however, the Court had rarely been concerned with the electoral or legislative process. During the 1960's the Warren Court turned the corner. The justices have now ruled, in constitutional terms, upon eligibility to vote, the apportionment of representatives, and even a State legislature's refusal to seat a successful candidate for office. One can only speculate how far the trend will carry — perhaps the litigation over the refusal of Congress to seat Adam Clayton Powell will provide an indication — but it seems clear that a majority of the present justices conceive it to be one of the self-conscious functions of constitutional adjudication to secure at least some of the basic democratic elements in the political process.

I

Chronologically the story begins with the Reapportionment Cases. *Baker* v. *Carr*[1] held that the Fourteenth Amendment's guarantee of "equal protection of the laws" gives each citizen an individual right to equal representation in a State legislature, which is enforceable by the federal judiciary. *Reynolds* v. *Sims*[2] and companion cases decided that whether one's representation is equal is to be measured, in the absence of exceptional circumstances, by the formula "one man, one vote" applied separately to each branch of a State legislature. The then-existing composition of five sixths of all State legislatures was rendered unconstitutional. Many States are still seeking to conform to the ruling. One consequence may be shifts in party power, but the real hope is that redistribution of seats to urban and suburban districts will revitalize State government.

The Reapportionment Cases raised with unique intensity the central question of constitutional adjudication—what is the proper role of the Supreme Court in American government? A Council of Wise Men, charged with doing whatever is good, or just, or wise, would have found no difficulty in voiding the apportionment of the Tennessee legislature which was at issue in *Baker* v. *Carr*. The people in some counties had eight, ten, and even twenty times as much representation, measured per capita, as the people in others. That was true in both Senate and House. Counties containing more than 60 percent of the population elected about a third of each house. The Tennessee legislature, by failing to make a per capita apportionment, had been violating Tennessee's own constitution for sixty years. No one would defend these inequities as a matter of sound government or abstract justice. Other State legislatures under rural domination, as in Tennessee, had failed to adapt themselves to the burgeoning problems of an urban, industrial society. There was loss of confidence in local government, coupled with an ever growing tendency to bypass State capitals in favor of national solutions. Reapportionment, though not a panacea, might bring new vigor to the State legislatures by making them more responsive to current needs.

But a court is subject to limitations not felt by a Council of Wise Men. Our constitutional system can work successfully only in a country where there is enormous respect for law and judicial decrees. Force is sometimes necessary to support constitutional mandates, as at Little Rock, Arkansas, and Oxford, Mississippi, but in the long run force cannot take the place of voluntary compliance in a society that values freedom. It is neither force nor the threat of punishment that makes a President who seizes the steel mills in time of crisis bow to the Supreme Court's decision that his action is illegal, nor does force or the threat of force induce the railroad employees to respect an order to abandon a strike. The power of legitimacy, which induces voluntary acceptance of Supreme Court decisions, rests largely upon the understanding that the justices are applying a law that binds them no less than the litigants—a general rule applicable to all men equally, yesterday, today, and tomorrow. Some measure of observance of this limitation is necessary, therefore, to the viability of a constitutionalism based upon judicial review.

If the need to follow an existing rule of law were controlling, there were major obstacles to judicial intervention in *Baker* v. *Carr*. Malapportionment, though it was growing demonstrably worse, had characterized one or both branches of most State legislatures from colonial times. The federal courts had not even been asked to intervene prior to 1940. Between 1946 and 1962 the Supreme Court had repeatedly declined the invitation.[3]

It was hard, moreover, to find reasonably objective standards by which a court could judge the fairness of any particular apportionment. Apart from the general guarantee of "equal protection of the law" no words in the Constitution, precedent, or accepted practice supplied a rule of decision. Perhaps one could fairly argue that the familiar principle condemning differentiations which lack any rational justification invalidates a crazy quilt like Tennessee's apportionment, which lacked both rhyme and reason, even though the principle had never been applied to elections. The next step would be to attempt to classify permissible and impermissible bases for differentiation. Race, religion, wealth, and occupation could well be said to be irrelevant to any *legitimate* purpose of apportionment, as could any weighting of rural or economic interest. But the very term "legitimate" requires a standard of legitimacy, and such policies as following the lines of political subdivisions, avoiding districts spread over large geographical areas, and even according representation to towns or counties rather than people could not be described as so irrational in all cases as to fall under the constitutional condemnation of arbitrary action.

In deciding whether an issue is justiciable one of the prime considerations is the ability of a court to frame and administer a suitable remedy. How could a court compel a legislature to lay out new districts? How could a court draw the district lines? Looking at the matter more broadly, judicial intervention into what was historically a partisan political question might well impair the Court's ultimate power to resolve other, more suitable cases. As Justice Frankfurter later put it in dissent: "The Court's authority—possessed of neither the purse nor the sword—ultimately rests on sustained public confidence in its moral sanction. Such feeling must be nourished by the Court's complete detachment . . . from political entanglements and by abstention from injecting itself into the clash of political forces in political settlements."[4]

Yet against these ingrained teachings of the lawyer's profession there stood the stark fact that the cancer of malapportionment would continue to grow unless the Court excised it. It would have been best for the States themselves to act, but most State legislators were more interested in self-perpetuation than electoral reform. No one could realistically suppose that Congress would grasp the nettle. As a practical matter, either the Court must act or nothing would be done.

Ideally, the federal judicial branch ought not to enlarge its own jurisdiction simply because Congress and State governments have failed to solve the problems confided to them. Most wrongs must find their remedies in other forums. Not all the business of government is constitutional law. The ideal remedy is to reform the delinquents. But government is more pragmatic than ideal. In a practical world there is, and I suspect has to be, a good deal of play in the joints. If one arm of government cannot or will not solve an insistent problem, the pressure falls upon another. Constitutional adjudication must recognize that the peculiar nature of the Court's business gives it a governmental function which cannot be wholly discharged without the simple inquiry, "which decision will be best for the country?" Much of the activism of the Warren Court, not only in reapportionment but in criminal law and race relations, is the consequence of the neglect of other agencies of government. Except when dealing with racial segregation, the Warren Court has been slower than the Fuller, White, and Taft Courts to upset a considered legislative resolution of an important public issue.

Two other factors, which operate in a variety of contexts, argued for judicial intervention in the Reapportionment Cases. First, the Court can seldom be wholly neutral upon the social, political, or philosophical questions underlying constitutional litigation. Its opinions shape as well as express our national ideals. The school desegregation decisions, for example, proved to be a tremendous moral force quite apart from the formal decrees. Second, just as a Supreme Court decision commands a measure of obedience because it is the law, so does the Court tend to give legitimacy to practices it leaves undisturbed. The declination of jurisdiction in the Reapportionment Cases could not have been wholly neutral. However skillfully the Court had dressed a decision not to deal with malapportionment in the language of jurisdiction, the outcome would have put some stamp of legality upon the evil in the eyes of laymen and legislators, even if not in the eyes of lawyers.

Although political perceptions without roots in conventional sources of law are inadequate for a staple diet of constitutional adjudication, important legal principles, both constitutional and other, have often been created by a judicial *coup de main.* There are times, as all lawyers know, when new legal norms may be made to embody our ideals rather than measure our shortcomings — to project the direction of American life rather than record it. Justice Douglas epitomized what the Court took to be the essential egalitarianism of our political development when he observed in *Gray* v. *Sanders:* "The conception of political equality from the Declaration of Independence, to Lincoln's Gettysburg Address, to the Fifteenth, Seventeenth and Nineteenth Amendments can mean only one thing — one person, one vote."[5] The power of the ruling in the Reapportionment Cases — their claim to be law — rests upon the accuracy of the Court's perception and upon its ability, by expressing the ideal, to command a national consensus.

The ruling has been unpopular among professional politicians. In the summer of 1964 only the threat of filibuster blocked legislation to bar its implementation. Senator Dirksen continued to press for a congressional resolution recommending a constitutional amendment. Recently the Congress seemed about to enact legislation postponing any obligation to reform congressional districts until 1970. Thirty-two State legislatures, only two less than the required number, have requested a constitutional convention.

Yet it seems unlikely that all this action by professional politicians has much support among the people. The state resolutions calling for a constitutional amendment appear to be the fruit of quiet lobbying instead of popular pressure. Politicians tend to worry about the unknown and therefore dislike any change that upsets the existing structure or sources of power. Lobbyists for special interests reputedly prefer the status quo because they find it easier to influence the votes necessary to defeat regulatory measures in legislatures where rural counties are heavily overrepresented. In Congress the Senate recently defeated the bill to postpone reapportionment of congressional districts, and at the end of 1967 the resolution calling for a constitutional amendment had not passed either chamber. Even Senator Dirksen proposed to undo the Supreme Court decisions only as applied to one house of a State legislature and only by introducing a few specific bases of apportionment other than population.

On the whole, the Court's perception seems accurate and its power to command a national consensus much greater than many people supposed. The popular support for the decisions may be partly due to the fact that the new departure has touched few people very closely or adversely, but it seems to be bottomed upon the fundamental political egalitarianism of the American people.

II

The Reapportionment Cases leave three major problems unsettled.

First, how strictly must a State adhere to the requirement of *per capita* equality? In *Swann* v. *Adams*[6] the Court invalidated an apportionment of the Florida legislature which adhered so closely to equality that the population of the most underrepresented district was only 10 percent above the ideal mean and the population of the most overrepresented districts was only 15 to 20 percent below it; a majority could not be formed in either house without including representatives from districts with 47 percent of the population. Prior to *Baker* v. *Carr* such an apportionment would have been hailed as extraordinarily equitable. The key to the decision appears to be that Florida offered no explanation for the variation from mathematical equality.

The legally acceptable variations are proving to be few. The desire to favor the urban interest, or the rural interest, or any other geographical or economic group, will not suffice. Nor will a desire to follow the analogy of the United States Senate by treating counties as if they were States and giving each county equal representation in one branch of the legislature. The analogy is unpersuasive because the federal plan rests upon specific constitutional provisions not qualified by the equal protection clause. Nor will history suffice. The argument based upon history has the fatal weakness that it seeks to defend, merely on the ground of long existence, apportionments which became built-in obstacles to the political flux by which new majorities shape laws and policies to new conditions. The reapportionment decisions evince not merely egalitarianism but the will to keep our society open to political change. Nor will the geographical size of a district and sparsity of its population justify departure from per capita equality. In the Court's view, modern methods of transportation and communication have destroyed the relevance of this element.

Apparently a State can justify some variation by showing that it based the boundaries of its representative and senatorial districts on existing governmental boundaries: by following county lines, or combining counties, or dividing a whole county into several districts. The opinion in *Reynolds* v. *Sims* notes several advantages of that procedure: it reduces the opportunities for gerrymandering; it recognizes the corporate governmental interests and responsibilities often vested in counties and other subdivisions; it takes account of the fact that subdivisions often are the basis of political organisms whose own political life would function less effectively if part were truncated and grafted upon another unit. Since existing governmental boundaries do not readily lend themselves to manipulating representation to favor special interests, it would be surprising if the Court condemned a plan of districting and apportionment which departed from per capita equality only to the extent necessary to avoid breaking up counties or towns and combining parts of several political subdivisions into single districts.

The second major question left open by the precedents is whether the "one man, one vote" rule applies to county commissions, city councils, school boards, and similar bodies. Putting aside agencies with limited functions, it is hard to see how the "one man, one vote" principle is logically any less applicable to a city council or county board of supervisors than to a legislature. The council or board usually has less legislative power, but this does not make inequalities in per capita representation unimportant. If it is argued that there is no need for judicial intervention because a fairly apportioned State legislature can correct malapportionment in any lesser subdivision where it is important, the answer is likely to be that the citizen's right to equal representation is personal. The real difference is that malapportionment in a city or county seldom results in giving political dominance to a class of voters wholly different from the class that would dominate with per capita distribution; and therefore it does not ordinarily create the evils at which the original decisions were directed. Furthermore, insistence upon per capita equality might seriously hamper efforts to merge existing units of local governments and thereby to conform the boundaries of political subdivisions to the ecology of metropolitan areas. The Court was noticeably cautious in declining to apply the "one man, one vote" rule to a Michigan county with very limited powers and in approving district residence requirements for members elected at large to the city council in Virginia Beach.[7] One suspects, however, that the claims of logical consistency will prevail over any differences in political policy and that the requirement of per capita equality will be extended to the composition of county and municipal bodies with legislative power. Should the Court so rule, in the cases currently awaiting decision, its decisions will impinge upon many more people and upset many more settled practices than the original cases involving only State legislatures and congressional districts. Perhaps the popular reaction will be less favorable.

The third major question left unanswered by the Reapportionment Cases is whether the Court will also seek to apply constitutional controls to gerrymandering. Drawing the boundaries of geographical districts seems far less amenable to constitutional adjudication than apportioning numbers of representatives to geographical districts, and thus far the Court has declined to intervene.[8]

III

For most of our history, control of the electoral franchise rested with the States. The Framers said nothing about the election of State officials. Quite obviously it never occurred to them that the federal government would ever have anything to do with the matter. With respect to the election of Representatives to Congress the original Constitution provided that the qualifications for voting should be the same as those necessary to vote for the most numerous branch of the State legislature. The Seventeenth Amendment extended the same rule to the election of Senators. In neither case has Congress chosen to exercise whatever power over voter-qualifications may be comprehended within the power to make regulations governing the time, place, and manner of holding the elections. Presidential electors, strangely enough, are to be chosen by each State in whatever manner its legislature shall provide. The general understanding that the Fourteenth Amendment did not confer the franchise upon Negroes also gave rise to the long-and-widely-held assumption that that amendment did not affect the right to vote. The Fifteenth Amendment merely barred racial discrimination without affecting State power over other qualifications. Until recently, therefore, neither constitutional adjudication nor congressional legislation played more than a negligible part in defining the electorate.

The Reapportionment Cases cleared the ground for more active intervention by the Supreme Court. Once it was decided that the Fourteenth Amendment condemns arbitrary discrimination by a State in apportioning representation among voters, the holding that arbitrary discrimination in conferring the franchise is likewise unconstitutional became inevitable. Only Justice Harlan protested "this further extension of federal judicial power into the political affairs of the States."[9] The implications of the extension are best revealed by two cases decided in the spring of 1966, *Harper* v. *Virginia Board of Elections* and *Katzenbach* v. *Morgan*.

In *Harper* v. *Virginia Board of Elections*[10] the Court invalidated the long-familiar and twice-upheld State laws that made payment of the poll tax a prerequisite to voting. The opinion of the Court, written by Justice Douglas, holds that the equal protection clause requires absolute equality for rich and poor in matters pertaining to the franchise: "Wealth, like race, creed, or color is not germane to one's ability to participate intelligently in the electoral process."

The central difficulty of the case, from the standpoint of the judicial function in constitutional adjudication, is emphasized by one of the interesting sidelights of recent terms of Court—the growing division between Justice Black and other justices who, together with him, used to be labeled the "activist wing." Critics have said that Justice Black's use of the "plain meaning of the words" and the historical evidence of original intent left too much scope for reading his own policy judgments into the Constitution, but, whether that view be wrong or right, no justice has ever tried more diligently to find what he regarded as objective standards of reference nor stressed more consistently the need for judicial restraint in the absence of an objective standard. In a biting dissent in the poll tax case, Justice Black criticized the tendency of "this Court to use the Equal Protection Clause, as it has today, to write into the Constitution its notions of what it thinks is good governmental policy."

The opinion of the Court is strangely open to this criticism. Except for reliance upon the Reapportionment Cases it seems almost perversely to repudiate every conventional guide to legal judgment. The language of the equal protection clause—a State may not deny to any person the "equal protection of the laws"—is obviously inconclusive; every law that results in treating some groups differently from others is not automatically unconstitutional. The evidence of original intent is flatly inconsistent with the theory that rich and poor must have an equal voice in elections, for the ownership of property was long regarded as a highly relevant qualification for voting as a measure of responsibility and material interest in government affairs. The poll tax itself was sanctioned by age, usage, and legal precedent.[11] Justice Douglas swept all this aside with this observation: "In determining what lines are unconstitutionally discriminatory, we have never been confined to historic notions of equality ... Notions of what constitutes equal treatment for purposes of the Equal Protection Clause *do* change." But the opinion does not say whence the Court is to derive its standards, beyond asserting: "Our conclusion is founded not on what we think governmental policy should be, but on what the Equal Protection Clause requires."

Such assertions are rather characteristic of the recent development of the equal protection clause. One element in the process of decision is evidently the relative invidiousness of the particular differentiation, such as that between men of different race, farmer and city-dweller, rich and poor, literate and illiterate, or men and women. The second element is the relative importance of the subject with respect to which equality is sought, such as the vote, the defense of a criminal prosecution, or civil litigation. But although one can identify the critical elements, the opinions do not succeed in elaborating a rational standard, or even points of reference, by which to judge in other cases what differentiations are permitted and when equality is required.

Perhaps this is because the Court is breaking new ground. One of the sources of creativity in adjudication according to the common-law method is that it permits the drawing of unifying and systematizing generalizations after the event on the basis of decisions which were initially rendered only upon intuitive perception of the wise and just result. One wonders, however, whether the difficulty of defining a rational standard is not more attributable to the fact that the very character of the judgment being exercised makes it unsuitable for adjudication in accordance with conventional legal methods.

Doubts upon this score may explain the emphasis which the Court has now placed upon the powers of Congress under Section 5 of the Fourteenth Amendment in the litigation over a New York statute that required a citizen to demonstrate his ability to read and understand English in order to vote. The requirement disenfranchised Puerto Ricans who had been educated in Spanish in Puerto Rican schools and had moved to New York where they lived without learning to read or write English. In *Cardona* v. *Power*[12] the appellant challenged the constitutionality of New York's differentiating English literacy from Spanish literacy for purposes of the franchise on the ground that it denied Spanish-speaking voters equal protection of the law. *Katzenbach* v. *Morgan*[13] put in issue the constitutionality of the relief that Congress sought to provide through a section of the Voting Rights Act of 1965, which enacted that no person who has successfully completed the sixth grade in a Puerto Rican school where instruction is in Spanish shall be denied the right to vote because of inability to read or write English. In *Morgan* the Court upheld the statutory enactment as a proper exercise of congressional power under Section 5 of the Fourteenth Amendment. In *Cardona,* which was decided the same day, it pretermitted the question whether the amendment invalidated New York's English literacy test without the aid of federal legislation.

The *Morgan* opinion has two branches. One upheld the power of Congress to extend the right to vote in New York elections to Spanish-speaking citizens from Puerto Rico as a means of reducing the danger that New York would fail to give them perfect equality of civil rights and equal protection of the law in accordance with the Fourteenth Amendment. The importance of this branch of the case lies outside the area of voting and is discussed in an earlier lecture.[14]

The second branch of the *Morgan* opinion upheld the constitutionality of Section 4(e) of the Voting Rights Act upon the alternative ground that: "[We] perceive a basis upon which Congress might predicate a judgment that the application of New York's English literacy requirement to deny the right to vote to a person with a sixth grade education in Puerto Rican schools . . . constituted an invidious discrimination in violation of the Equal Protection Clause."

This rationale introduces a strikingly novel form of judicial deference to congressional power. The substance of the holding is that Congress may decide, within broad limits, how the general principle of equal protection applies to actual conditions. One dramatic consequence, as Justice Harlan pointed out in dissent, is that Congress can invalidate a State enactment upon the ground that it denies equal protection where the Court would uphold, or even has upheld, the constitutionality of the same enactment.

Yet the decision follows logically from familiar principles and should prove a happy innovation, relieving pressures upon the Court. Whether a State law denies equal protection depends to a large extent upon finding and appraising the practical importance of relevant facts—in the case of the English literacy requirement, upon such considerations as the extent to which the requirement served as an incentive to learn English and ease the process of assimilation, the availability of Spanish-language newspapers and their sufficiency to enable non-English-speaking voters to exercise the franchise intelligently, the importance of the franchise, and the relative effectiveness of other inducements to learn English. There is often room for differences of opinion in interpreting the available data. *A fortiori* men may differ upon the values of competing desiderata. The accepted principle of constitutional review is that the Court should assume that there are facts which furnish a constitutional foundation for the State legislation unless that conclusion is rationally impossible. Section 5 of the Fourteenth Amendment, as here interpreted, gives Congress concurrent power to invalidate State legislation. Under other articles the Court is also committed to a presumption that facts exist which sustain congressional legislation, and to deference to congressional judgment upon questions of degree and proportion. In the *Morgan* case the conflicting federal and State statutes appeared to rest upon inconsistent legislative findings and evaluations of the underlying conditions. The Court, applying the rule of deference to Congress, found the federal enactment valid and required the State to yield. Justice Harlan would have held that "in the area of primary state concern a state statute that passes constitutional muster under the judicial standard of rationality should not be set at naught by a mere contrary congressional pronouncement unsupported by a legislative record justifying that conclusion." In my view Justice Brennan had the better of the argument. To recognize that Congress has supremacy over the judiciary in the areas of legislative fact-finding, and that Congress' findings must prevail over those of the State legislatures in any area within federal power, seems more consonant with the predominant themes of our constitutional history than judicially defined areas of primary and secondary State and federal competence.

The *Morgan* case opens the constitutional door for new federal legislation designed to relax State qualifications for voting and achieve greater uniformity. If Congress can make a conclusive legislative finding that ability to read and write English, as distinguished from Spanish, is constitutionally irrelevant to voting, then a finding that all literacy requirements are barriers to equality might be equally conclusive. Congress would seem to have power to make a similar finding about State laws denying the franchise to persons eighteen, nineteen, and twenty years old even though they work, pay taxes, raise families, and are subject to military service. The constitutionality of federal prescription of residence requirements may be more doubtful because the differentiations made by State laws are more difficult to characterize as invidious, but it would seem that much of President Johnson's desire for expansion of the electorate could be realized by legislation without a constitutional amendment. Whether Congress is prepared to exert its power thus to nationalize the rules governing the franchise is quite a different question. Here as elsewhere, its temper is more traditional than the Court's.

IV

A more recent indication of the Court's own attitude towards the extension of federal constitutional control over the electoral process is found in *Fortson* v. *Morris,*[15] a case growing out of Georgia's 1966 gubernatorial election. Callaway obtained 47.07 percent of the popular vote; Maddox received 46.88 percent, and Arnall 6.05 percent. The Georgia constitution provided that when no candidate obtained a majority in the popular election, the legislature should elect the Governor from the two persons who received the highest number of votes. A three-judge federal district court enjoined the legislature from making its election on the ground that this provision denied Georgia voters equal protection of the law. The Supreme Court reversed. Five justices held that, since Georgia could constitutionally choose her governor through the legislature instead of by popular election, there was no constitutional barrier to use of that method when no candidate received a majority of the popular vote. Justice Douglas, in a dissent joined by the Chief Justice and Justices Brennan and Fortas, argued that once a popular election was held the office could not constitutionally go to the candidate who ran second. Justice Fortas, with whom the Chief Justice and Justice Douglas concurred, pressed the further observation that the constitutionality of electing a governor through the legislature should not "be cavalierly assumed."

The decision seemingly involved a deliberate choice not to extend the Reapportionment Cases. In *Gray* v. *Sanders*[16] the Court had invalidated the county unit system for nominating candidates for statewide office. Under that system each county was allotted an arbitrary number of votes, unrelated to population and designed to preserve the rural counties' political hegemony. The popular vote, counted county by county, determined how the unit votes should be cast, but a candidate receiving the largest number of popular votes would lose to a candidate receiving a majority of the units. In the run-off election case the dissenters claimed that if the legislature were allowed to choose the second highest candidate, the popular votes "would be weighted contrary to the principle of 'one person, one vote.'" The argument depends upon the unarticulated assumption that representatives in the legislature are reflecting the votes of their constituents when they perform their own duties. The assumption seems unsound. Although political practice has retreated far down that road since Edmund Burke delivered his famous Address to the Electors of Bristol, constitutional doctrine does not yet deny that representatives are free to exercise independent judgment. The stronger argument was that the decision in the *Gray* v. *Sanders* county unit case rested upon the proposition that the Fourteenth Amendment gives a majority (or perhaps a plurality) of the voters the substantive right to elect the governor, at least when they are permitted to vote. The majority rejected this interpretation; it read *Gray* v. *Sanders* as holding only that a State violates the Fourteenth Amendment when it gives a minority of its people more political power than the majority, because of the unequal treatment thus accorded equally qualified voters. Either reading is consistent with familiar judicial method. The law often grows by finding broader principles implicit in a narrow precedent, but it is equally permissible to confine a precedent to the narrowest generalization derivable from the facts. The important point is that a majority of the justices, when given the alternatives, chose not to expand constitutional supervision of State elections into an area in which a contrary decision would have had no support in the words of the document.

The most expansive opinion was delivered by Justice Fortas. Using the rhetoric of understatement, he argued for a reading of the Reapportionment Cases that would require the popular election of governors: "Their meaning and thrust are perhaps deeper than the mechanics of the tally. They are, one may hope, not merely much ado about form. They represent, one has been led to believe, an acknowledgment that the Republican form of government guaranteed by the Constitution, read in light of the General Welfare Clause, the guaranties of equal protection of the laws and the privileges and immunities of citizens of the United States, requires something more than an adherence to form . . . Today's decision is a startling reversal; a belittling, I say with all respect, of our Constitution's dynamic provisions with respect to the basic instrument of democracy — the vote."

Few judicial opinions, even in dissent, claim for the Supreme Court as expansive and free-wheeling a role in supervising the structure of State governments as the passage just quoted. As late as *Baker* v. *Carr* the Court had approved earlier decisions holding that the vague contours of the constitutional guarantee of a "republican form of government" are not susceptible of judicial enforcement.[17] To expand this vague declaration still further "in light of the General Welfare Clause" is to ignore all constitutional charts and sail whatever course the judge thinks will be in the public weal. (Of course, the general welfare clause says nothing about the powers of the Supreme Court or the form of State government. It provides that Congress may lay and collect taxes, and pay the debts and provide for the common defense and general welfare of the United States.) Dissenting rhetoric is often unrestrained but it is well to remember, before brushing this view aside, that time has a way of converting the dissenting views of a vigorous junior justice into the opinions of the Court.

Fortson v. *Morris* is thus a useful reminder that thus far the Warren Court has not been unmindful of both branches of the antinomy that lies at the heart of constitutional adjudication. Its creativity seems virtually unprecedented, but here, as in the sit-in cases and in its effort to avoid direct conflicts with considered legislative judgments, the Court has recognized that there are limits to what can be accomplished by constitutional adjudication without undue risk of undermining the rule of law.

Only history will know whether the Warren Court has struck the balance right. For myself, I am confident that historians will write that the trend of decisions during the 1950's and 1960's was in keeping with the mainstream of American history—a bit progressive but also moderate, a bit humane but not sentimental, a bit idealistic but seldom doctrinaire, and in the long run essentially pragmatic—in short, in keeping with the true genius of our institutions.

But my view is deeply prejudiced. One who has sat in the Supreme Court almost daily awaiting oral argument or the delivery of opinions acquires both admiration and affection for the Court and for all the justices. The problems with which they deal are so difficult, the number and variety of cases are so overwhelming, the implications are so far-reaching, that one sits humbled by the demands upon them. That the institution of constitutional adjudication works so well on the whole is testimony not only to the genius of the institution but to the wisdom and courage of the individual justices.

Notes

1 The Basic Dilemma

1. 1 Cranch 137 (1803).
2. 347 U.S. 483 (1954).
3. 372 U.S. 368 (1963).
4. 376 U.S. 1 (1964).
5. 377 U.S. 533 (1964).
6. 383 U.S. 663 (1966).
7. Id. at 668.
8. 351 U.S. 12 (1956).
9. 372 U.S. 335 (1963).
10. 372 U.S. 353 (1963).
11. Id. at 357.
12. 376 U.S. 254 (1964).
13. Gideon v. Wainwright, 372 U.S. 335 (1963).
14. Mapp v. Ohio, 367 U.S. 643 (1961).
15. Escobedo v. Illinois, 378 U.S. 478 (1964); Miranda v. Arizona 384 U.S. 436 (1966).
16. Silverman v. United States, 365 U.S. 505 (1961); Osborn v. United States, 385 U.S. 323 (1966); Berger v. New York, 388 U.S. 41 (1967).
17. 376 U.S. 254 (1964).
18. Time, Inc. v. Hill, 385 U.S. 374 (1966).
19. Linn v. Plant Guard Workers, 383 U.S. 53 (1966).
20. Civil Rights Cases, 109 U.S. 3 (1883).
21. 384 U.S. 641 (1966).
22. 383 U.S. 745 (1966).

23. Shuttlesworth v. City of Birmingham, 382 U.S. 87 (1965).
24. Cox v. Louisiana, 379 U.S. 536 (1965).
25. Watkins v. United States, 354 U.S. 178 (1957); Sweezy v. New Hampshire, 354 U.S. 234 (1957).
26. Katzenbach v. McClung, 379 U.S. 294 (1964).
27. Dombrowski v. Pfister, 380 U.S. 479 (1965).
28. 310 U.S. 88, 97-98 (1940).
29. Barrows v. Jackson, 346 U.S. 249 (1953); Nat'l. Ass'n. for the Advancement of Colored People v. Alabama, 357 U.S. 449 (1958).
30. Mitchell v. United States, cert. denied, 386 U.S. 972 (1967); Mora v. McNamara, cert. denied, 36 U.S.L.W. 3189 (U.S. Nov. 6, 1967).
31. L. Hand, *Mr. Justice Cardozo,* 52 Harv. L. Rev. 361 (1939). Copyright 1939 by The Harvard Law Review Association.

2   *Civil Rights: Judicial Innovation*

1. 347 U.S. 483 (1954).
2. 163 U.S. 537 (1896).
3. 109 U.S. 3 (1883).
4. Burton v. Wilmington Parking Authority, 365 U.S. 715, 722 (1961).
5. 334 U.S. 1, 19-20 (1948).
6. Garner v. Louisiana, 368 U.S. 157, 176 (1961); Lombard v. Louisiana, 373 U.S. 267, 274 (1963).
7. 345 U.S. 461 (1953).
8. 326 U.S. 501 (1946).
9. 365 U.S. 715 (1961).
10. Id. at 725.
11. Griffin v. Illinois, 351 U.S. 12 (1956).
12. Garner v. Louisiana, 368 U.S. 157 (1961).
13. Edwards v. South Carolina, 372 U.S. 229 (1963).
14. Peterson v. City of Greenville, 373 U.S. 244 (1963); Lombard v. Louisiana, 373 U.S. 267 (1963).
15. Hamm v. City of Rock Hill, 379 U.S. 306 (1964).
16. 382 U.S. 296 (1966).
17. 387 U.S 369 (1967).

3   Civil Rights: Legislative Power

1. Katzenbach v. McClung, 379 U.S. 294 (1964).

2. NLRB v. Jones & Laughlin Steel Corp., 301 U.S. 1 (1937); Wickard v. Filburn, 317 U.S. 111 (1942).

3. Stafford v. Wallace, 258 U.S. 495 (1922); Chicago Bd. of Trade v. Olsen, 262 U.S. 1 (1923).

4. United States v. Darby, 312 U.S. 100 (1941).

5. Champion v. Ames, 188 U.S. 321 (1903).

6. Brennan's French Restaurant, 129 N.L.R.B. 52 (1960).

7. Mitchell v. United States, 313 U.S. 80 (1941); Boynton v. Virginia, 364 U.S. 454 (1960).

8. Civil Rights Cases, 109 U.S. 3 (1883).

9. United States v. Cruikshank, 92 U.S. 542 (1875); United States v. Harris, 106 U.S. 629 (1882).

10. Brief for Defendant at 75, South Carolina v. Katzenbach, 383 U.S. 301 (1966), quoting United States v. Darby, 312 U.S. 100, 121 (1941).

11. McCulloch v. Maryland, 4 Wheat. 316, 421 (1819).

12. 384 U.S. 641 (1966).

13. Id. at 652-653.

14. United States v. Price, 383 U.S. 787 (1966).

15. Kasper v. Brittain, 245 F.2d 92 (6th Cir.), cert. denied, 355 U.S. 834 (1957); Bullock v. United States, 265 F.2d 683 (6th Cir.), cert. denied, 360 U.S. 909, 932 (1959); Brewer v. Hoxie School District No. 46, 238 F.2d 91 (8th Cir. 1956).

16. Katzenbach v. Morgan, 384 U.S. 641, 653 (1966).

17. See, e.g., Gideon v. Wainwright, 372 U.S. 335 (1963); Miranda v. Arizona, 384 U.S. 436 (1966).

18. 383 U.S. 745 (1966).

19. Id. at 753.

20. Id. at 762.

21. United States v. Cruikshank, 92 U.S. 542 (1875); United States v. Harris, 106 U.S. 629 (1882).

22. See footnote 15, supra.

23. United States v. Waddell, 112 U.S. 76 (1884).

24. N.L.R.B. v. Jones & Laughlin Steel Corp., 301 U.S. 1 (1937); Wickard v. Filburn, 317 U.S. 111 (1942).

25. Slaughter House Cases, 16 Wall. 36 (1873).

26. 109 U.S. 3 (1883).

27. Panhandle Oil Co. v. Mississippi ex rel. Knox, 277 U.S. 218, 223 (1928).

28. Schechter Poultry Corp. v. United States, 295 U.S. 495 (1935).

29. 301 U.S. 1 (1937).

30. Gibbons v. Ogden, 9 Wheat. 1, 197 (1824).

4   The Reform of Criminal Procedure

1. 302 U.S. 319 (1937).

2. 332 U.S. 46, 68 (1947).

3. See, e.g., Malloy v. Hogan, 378 U.S. 1 (1964).

4. See, e.g., Betts v. Brady, 316 U.S. 455 (1942).

5. Gideon v. Wainwright, 372 U.S. 335 (1963).

6. Griffin v. Illinois, 351 U.S. 12 (1956).

7. Douglas v. California, 372 U.S. 353 (1963).

8. Mapp v. Ohio, 367 U.S. 643 (1961).

9. Aguilar v. Texas, 378 U.S. 108 (1964).

10. Griffin v. California, 380 U.S. 609 (1965).

11. Escobedo v. Illinois, 378 U.S. 478 (1964); Miranda v. Arizona, 384 U.S. 436 (1966).

12. Osborn v. United States, 385 U.S. 323 (1966); Berger v. New York, 388 U.S. 41 (1967).

13. Brady v. Maryland, 373 U.S. 83 (1963); Giles v. Maryland, 386 U.S. 66 (1967).

14. Arnold v. North Carolina, 376 U.S. 773 (1964); Coleman v. Alabama, 377 U.S. 129 (1964).

15. Douglas v. Alabama, 380 U.S. 415 (1965); Pointer v. Texas, 380 U.S. 400 (1965).

16. Washington v. Texas, 388 U.S. 14 (1967).

17. In re Gault, 387 U.S. 1 (1967).

18. Olmstead v. United States, 277 U.S. 438 (1928).

19. See, e.g., Goldman v. United States, 316 U.S. 129 (1942).

20. 302 U.S. 379 (1937).

21. 373 U.S. 427 (1963).

22. Osborn v. United States, 385 U.S. 323 (1966).

23. 388 U.S. 41 (1967).

24. Id. at 70, 81.

25. 384 U.S. 436 (1966).

26. Brown v. Mississippi, 297 U.S. 278 (1936); Ashcraft v. Tennessee, 322 U.S. 143 (1944); Spano v. New York, 360 U.S. 315 (1959); Haynes v. Washington, 373 U.S. 503 (1963).

27. Gideon v. Wainwright, 372 U.S. 335 (1963).

28. Griffin v Illinois, 351 U.S. 12 (1956).

29. Camara v. Municipal Court ot the City and County of San Francisco, 387 U.S. 523 (1967).

30. Miranda v. Arizona, 384 U.S. 436, 504 (1966); In re Gault, 387 U.S. 1, 65 (1967).

31. See, e.g., In re Gault, 387 U.S. 1 (1967); United States v. Wade, 388 U.S. 218 (1967).

32. Berger v. New York, 388 U.S. 41, 89 (1967).

33. 384 U.S. 436, 467, 490 (1966).

5   *Political Democracy: Speech and Association*

1. 1 Annals of Cong. 439 (1789).

2. Prudential Ins. Co. of America v. Cheek, 259 U.S. 530 (1922).

3. United States v. Carolene Products Co., 304 U.S. 144, 152 (1938).

4. Garrison v. Louisiana, 379 U.S. 64, 74-75 (1964).

5. Brennan, *The Supreme Court and the Meiklejohn Interpretation of the First Amendment,* 79 Harv. L. Rev. 1 (1965). Copyright 1965 by The Harvard Law Review Association.

6. Dennis v. United States, 341 U.S. 494 (1951).

7. Time, Inc. v. Hill, 385 U.S. 374 (1967).

8. Id. at 387-388.

9. Melvin v. Reid, 112 Cal. App. 285, 297 P. 91 (1931).

10. 385 U.S. at 383-384.

11. See, e.g., Justice Brennan dissenting opinion in Lopez v. United States, 373 U.S. 427, 449-450 (1963).

12. 385 U.S. at 388.

13. 357 U.S. 449 (1958).

14. 361 U.S. 516 (1960).

15. Keyishian v. Board of Regents, 385 U.S. 589 (1967).

16. 342 U.S. 485 (1952).

17. Adderly v. Florida, 385 U.S. 39, 49-50 (1966) (dissenting opinion).

18. 379 U.S. 536 (1965).

19. Ibid.

20. Edwards v. South Carolina, 372 U.S. 229 (1963).

21. Cox v. Louisiana, 379 U.S. 536 (1965).

22. Ibid.

23. Watkins v. United States, 354 U.S. 178 (1957); United States v. Rumely, 345 U.S. 41 (1953).

24. 383 U.S. 131 (1966).

25. 385 U.S. 39 (1966).

6 Political Democracy: Voting Rights and Legislative Apportionment

1. 369 U.S. 186 (1962).

2. 377 U.S. 533 (1964).

3. Colegrove v. Green, 328 U.S. 549 (1946). Other cases are collected in *Baker* v. *Carr,* 369 U.S. 186, 270 n.l.

4. Baker v. Carr, 369 U.S. 186, 267 (1962).

5. 372 U.S. 368, 381 (1963).

6. Swann v. Adams, 385 U.S. 440 (1967).

7. Dusch v. Davis, 387 U.S. 112 (1967).

8. Cf. Wright v. Rockefeller, 376 U.S. 52 (1964).

9. Carrington v. Rash, 380 U.S. 89, 98 (1965).

10. 383 U.S. 663 (1966).

11. Breedlove v. Suttles, 302 U.S. 277 (1937); Butler v. Thompson, 341 U.S. 937 (1951).

12. 384 U.S. 672 (1966).

13. 384 U.S. 641 (1966).

14. See pages 57-60 supra.

15. 385 U.S. 231 (1966).

16. 372 U.S. 368 (1963).

17. Pacific States Telephone and Telegraph Co. v. Oregon, 223 U.S. 118 (1912); Baker v. Carr 369 U.S. 186, 223 (1962).

Index

Harvard Paperbacks

1   **The United States and China**   *Third edition*   John King Fairbank

2   **Three Thousand Years of Educational Wisdom:** Selections from Great Documents   *Second edition, enlarged*   Robert Ulich, editor

3   **Earth, Moon, and Planets**   *Third edition*   Fred L. Whipple

4   **The Ideological Origins of the American Revolution**   Bernard Bailyn

5   **Notes on the Synthesis of Form**   Christopher Alexander

6   **Blacks in Antiquity:** Ethiopians in the Greco-Roman Experience   Frank M. Snowden, Jr.

7   **On Extended Wings:** Wallace Stevens' Longer Poems   Helen Hennessy Vendler

8   **Dissent in Three American Wars**   Samuel Eliot Morison, Frederick Merk, and Frank Freidel

9   **Set Theory and Its Logic**   *Revised edition*   Willard Van Orman Quine

10   **Marihuana Reconsidered**   Lester Grinspoon

11   **The Functions of the Executive**   Chester I. Barnard

12   **Never in Anger:** Portrait of an Eskimo Family   Jean L. Briggs

13   **The Soviet Bloc:** Unity and Conflict   *Revised and enlarged edition*   Zbigniew K. Brzezinski

14   **The Renaissance of the Twelfth Century**   Charles Homer Haskins

15   **Eleanor of Aquitaine and the Four Kings**   Amy Kelly

16   **The Copernican Revolution:** Planetary Astronomy in the Development of Western Thought   Thomas S. Kuhn

17   **Philosophy in a New Key:** A Study in the Symbolism of Reason, Rite, and Art   *Third edition*   Susanne K. Langer

18   **The Great Chain of Being:** A Study of the History of an Idea   Arthur O. Lovejoy

19   **Populations, Species, and Evolution:** An Abridgment of *Animal Species and Evolution*   Ernst Mayr

20   **The Transcendentalists:** An Anthology   Perry Miller, editor

21   **Virgin Land:** The American West as Symbol and Myth   Henry Nash Smith

22   **Music and Imagination**   Aaron Copland

23   **i: Six Nonlectures**   E. E. Cummings